The Growing Christian

Two Paths of the Christian Belief

THE GROWING CHRISTIAN

TWO PATHS OF THE CHRISTIAN BELIEF

Rebekah Van Natta

LORD
AND
ARMOR

The Growing Christian
Two Paths of the Christiain Belief

Author: Rebekah Van Natta
Cover Art by: Dijan Gmizovic

Published by Lord and Armor
www.lordandarmor.com

Published in the United States of America

ISBN: 979-8-9905038-0-9

Contents

Acknowledgments

It's amazing how many times I've tried to sit down to write a book and have never been able to finish. This is hopefully one book of many to come! There are a few people I need to thank.

First off, GOD. Thank you for coming into my life and transforming my heart and my mind, I feel renewed, and alive for the first time in my life. When I sat down to write, I prayed for the Holy Spirit to guide me, and I believe he did. I pray this book blesses whoever reads it and I'm so grateful that you allowed your truth to be used through my writing.

Secondly, I'd like to thank my husband Andy for always encouraging me to conquer all my dreams and also for inspiring me to write this book. You've always challenged me, pushed me, motivated me, and you've always been my biggest fan and cheerleader, I love you!

Dana- Sue, I could not have done this without you! Who knew over a decade later that we would be working together through our connection of my mother "Super Sue"? Thank you for your guidance, your expertise, and your willingness to help make my dream of getting this book out in the world come true. God is so awesome in how he works, and how he connects people. I am so grateful for you, love you!

I also want to thank my mother for always being a light in my life, my motivation, my inspiration. My life is what it is because of the legacy you've left behind, and although I miss you everyday you're not with us, you have been so present in everything I do, I love you.

Dad and Rachel, I love you both. Thank you for always being a part of my journey. All my big ideas and wild dreams, you guys have been so encouraging, patient, and loving. You both rock my world in so many ways, theres no words to describe my love for the two of you.

A Personal Note

The reason I wrote this book was to reveal to believers the true walk with Christ and not just their belief of what walking with Christ looks like. This comes from my personal experience of living a Christian life and realizing I was living more of a "Rebekah" life than a "God" life. My journey has just started, so everything I've written applies to my daily life in walking closer with the Lord. I never knew the true power and freedom of the Lord until I turned completely to Him. The more I started sharing my new relationship in Jesus with others, the more I realized a need for a book like this. It's really easy to conform with the world, with our without knowing. I'm hoping this book is able to give you a few tools to help guide you in your walk with Jesus. Writing this book has also allowed me to further seek after the Lord and to also hold me accountable in my walk with Him. My hope for myself and for you is to be able to know God truly and to follow Him deeply.

With Love,

Rebekah Van Natta

THE GROWING CHRISTIAN

TWO PATHS OF THE CHRISTIAN BELIEF

A Prayer for You

Dear Lord,

I pray this book brings truth and light to whoever is reading. Let them feel your presence as they read and meditate on the words you've put in my heart to share. Remind them how much you love them in this moment and throughout their read. If there are any moments where they need to ask for your help whether to repent, or forgive someone Lord, I ask you give them the strength to do so. Allow them to lean on you as you walk with them in their faith journey. Bless them for being curious to know you more and let them know you are always with them. Amen.

INTRODUCTION

Being a believer in Christ is a complex, ongoing journey marked by questions, doubts, and a deep longing to understand the nature of God. It is also an ongoing journey of you, yourself changing, being molded, and crafted into the person God has created for you to be. You might often think, what am I doing in this world? What is my purpose? What are my gifts? Does God really love me? Can God really use me? Why does God allow pain and suffering? Where was God when I needed him? I believe in God, but… I believe in God, however… I can relate with all these questions because I'm human too. I live in the real world full of both light and dark, good and evil. I'm sure you've experienced your "Why God" moment by now. Maybe you've had a few. I grew up with a wonderful mom and dad. I had a great childhood, lots of love, support, opportunities, and friends. I look back at my younger life and often think wow, how lucky was I - I had it all! I mean growing up in the 90's was a good time to be a kid! However, when I hit my 20's, my life drastically changed. I went through the hardest, most difficult years of my life and I found myself questioning God and my purpose almost daily. I will tell you that I truly believed in God. I always have, I prayed to God, I loved God, but I didn't know God.

Does that even make sense? How can you believe in something, love something, and not know it? My focus, my priority, my desires, and dreams all revolved around me, not God. Nowhere in my day or even in mind was my priority, thankfulness, or focus set on God. When you start spending time in The Word and with God, it's crazy how your world literally turns upside down in such a good way. Somehow everything changes and your eyes are truly opened to seeing the Truth. Not the world's truth but, Gods Truth.

In John 8:31-32 Jesus says to his disciples, "If you continue in My word, you are truly My disciples. Then you will know the truth, and the truth will set you free."

Romans 8:2 "For in Christ Jesus the law of the Spirit of life (Jesus) set you free from the law of sin and death (the world, your flesh)."

These are God's words from yes, the Bible. Christians and believers know this, but do we really live into it? I mean, do we truly trust His words, read and meditate on His words, and have childlike faith in His words? I never gave the Bible much thought other than it was a historical book full of stories and life lessons. I wasn't even sure I believed it was all true! So, what are these two paths of the Christian belief? There are believers who believe in Christ but are not seeking or walking with Him daily, and there are believers who believe in Christ who are choosing to seek Him daily, ultimately dying to themselves daily in order to walk with Him. Let me clarify and bring light to one thing. If you're a believer in Christ and you have given your life to Him, you are His no matter what!

> ***Deuteronomy 31:8 "The LORD himself goes before you and will be with you; he will never leave you nor forsake you. Do not be afraid; do not be discouraged."***

Just because you've gone astray doesn't mean God forgets about you or leaves you. Remember God is our Shepherd, and we are His sheep. In general, when a single sheep loses his way and gets lost, the Shepherd doesn't just let the sheep go to tend to the rest of his flock. He leaves his entire flock and goes to find the one sheep who is lost. When He finds the sheep, He rejoices and carries it back to his flock.

> ***Isaiah 53:6 "We all, like sheep, have gone astray, each of us has turned to our own way; and the LORD has laid on him the iniquity of us all."***

Jesus paid it all for us! Every sin each one of us commits known or unknown Jesus laid down his perfect life, a life none of us could ever have lived and He did it for us. God loves us so much, that He didn't want to be separated from us, His children. So, He sent himself. He sent Jesus to cleanse us of our sins so that one day, when this life is over, we can be reunited with Him. It's hard to imagine a love that big! In this short book, we'll dive a little deeper into the two paths of the Christian belief: The Believer Not the Seeker, and The Believer Who Seeks. We all have questions naturally, but at what point do we surrender those questions to God and decide that getting to know Him matters more? After all, He is God, right? He is all knowing, The Creator, The Beginning, and the End, The Omega, The Word, The Almighty, God with us. But could one path bring us true freedom in an individual's faith journey more than the other? I believe when you're done reading this book, you'll want to know God more than you question Him and seek Him more than just believe in Him. Let's explore.

CHAPTER 1
My Why God Moment

CHAPTER 1
My Why God Moment

At the age of 21, I lost my mother to breast cancer. It was Stage 4 Invasive Breast Cancer, and she passed away within five months of being diagnosed. Five months from the time I found out she wasn't well, 'til the time she was gone, it doesn't give one much, if anytime, to fully process a death. My world was shattered and my future, which looked so colorful, now looked like a blank canvas. I was just stepping into adulthood, I thought I had all the time in the world. I thought there was plenty of time to have my mom be my friend, my mentor, my adulting resource to go to, and just like that it was gone. All the joys to come in my young growing life, to find love, get married, and have children now looked different without her in the picture. My mom was the glue, she was our foundation, our light, and now that light and even our hope had been extinguished.

A Little About Mom

To fully understand the remarkable woman my mother was, it is important to know that she was affectionately known as "Super Sue" by her clients, friends, and her children. She was a powerhouse, a beacon of strength, hope and light, a dedicated wife, mother, and friend. She was a registered nurse, but decided to change her occupation into a more holistic approach where she managed her own successful business as an Integrated Reflexologist. She devoted her spare time to the YMCA, where she taught an array of fitness classes along with leading the run club. My mother was a marathoner and triathlete among many other big accomplishments in the fitness world. She was God's biggest fan and loved by so many for her big heart. In addition, she achieved incredible accomplishments, including the completion of over 30 marathons while qualifying for the Boston Marathon every time (and here I am just trying to keep my mile under 9 minutes!). She conquered numerous triathlons, 100-mile canoe races, 200-mile relay runs, and century bike rides. Somehow, amidst all of this, she still managed to pour her heart into the lives of those she loved, always going above and beyond. Her love for people radiated, making the world a better place in her presence. Going back to mom's astonishing accomplishments, it was never just about crossing those finish lines; it was about running each race for a greater cause and purpose.

My mother was deeply committed to Team In Training (TNT), a nonprofit organization dedicated to fighting Leukemia & Lymphoma. Her journey with TNT was remarkable, having raised an astounding $100,000 on her own, solidifying her status as one of the top fundraisers for the Texas Gulf Coast Team. I have many memories of her half marathons and marathons starting back when I was just nine years old. The image of hot cocoa and donuts comes to mind as we cheered her on. My dad tracking her miles and all of us jumping in the car to head to her next mile marker so we could cheer her on throughout the entire race all the way to the finish line. Her passion extended beyond the finish line, as she would proudly display her patients' faces and names on her jersey, encouraging support and cheers to help them battle their own challenges. My mother Sue's charisma, perseverance, and unwavering spirit left a permanent mark on everyone she touched - not only was she strong and determined, but a force of hope.

Mom's battle with cancer ended far too soon. A healthy, strong, fit, kind, loving woman who lived her life for God and others diagnosed with Stage 4 Invasive Breast Cancer and then five months later, just gone. It wasn't fair! It left me and our entire family shattered, lost, and broken. Cancer…I hate it. Not only does it confine its cruelty to the individual suffering - it reaches out and touches everyone who knows them. THIS was my WHY GOD moment. Why did you take her? Why did she have to suffer? Why did you allow this? All she did was love you and love people. Why!? What am I supposed to do now God? I remember those days of helplessness, the overwhelming sense of loss, and the emptiness that engulfed me. I struggled - physically, emotionally, mentally, spiritually, and financially. My faith was tested, my health deteriorated, and my resources were hardly enough to pay the bills. I felt like I lost my entire family in the matter of minutes! My dad was broken, lost and distant, my sister didn't know how to talk to me about anything. I was alone. I was far from okay. I felt like I was in a bad nightmare and all I wanted to do was wake up. I was so unsure of everything! During this dark and lonely time and what felt like forever, I was in desperate need of God, but I didn't realize that then. Over the course of a decade, I slowly found my way back to life, navigating through the seasons of grief and loss, learning to accept what was, what is and allowing myself to move forward.

However, life was still hard… really hard. Through a series of choices some good and some bad, my life led me down a path where I found success as an entrepreneur. I was living with my boyfriend who was going through a mid-life crisis and his four-year-old son. I wasn't going to church on a regular basis. I was drinking way too much and way too often, and I felt like I was the replacement of my mother just trying to keep my family taken care of and together. I was exhausted, I was sick all the time, I was emotionally, physically, and mentally drained. I was trying to do everything on my own. Thankfully God in His loving way, helped me through the hard times, even though I was far from Him. My boyfriend eventually became my husband, who is my best friend, and my business partner. I go to an amazing church where I feel God's presence, I cut way back on drinking, my family makes efforts to stay close and connected and they're all super happy and doing well! I'm finally fueled up and ready for whatever God brings my way!

The Shift

I don't know how it happened, but one day something was telling me to be still. This happened just about two years ago, at the age of 33, 12 years after mom passing. This wasn't the first or the second time I had felt the need for stillness, but this time, I did something different, I listened. Then "something" told me to be still and pray, so I did. I didn't even connect that it was God talking to me. I just felt "something". So, I asked God if it was Him, and if so, I told Him I needed help from Him in changing my heart because I knew I could not do it on my own. I had tried so many times to seek God, but always would fall back into the same routine and neglect time with Him. I had stopped going to church after mom died. It was too hard. She was always in the front row with her hands raised up, writing notes in her Bible, taking us over to the prayer corner for prayer. I had attended church here and there over the years but never committed or stuck to it. So, as I continued daily to spend a few minutes with God, I asked Him to change my heart… and He did.

Ironically, He changed my ears first. Immediately, I was very sensitive to the music I once listened to and the words that I would say. I had to completely change my genre of music from worldly, secular music to Christian music. Nothing was pleasant to listen to, but worship music. It was so crazy to me!

Dust Off Your Bible

Then I felt Him telling me to read the Bible. I thought, "seriously that old thing, how boring!" It took me a few days to find my Bible. I can't tell you the last time I actually read from it. I even called my dad to ask him where to start. I mean the bible is pretty big! He told me to start in the New Testament and get to know Jesus. When I have conversations with clients and friends about reading the Bible and they ask where to start, I just repeat what my dad said! The Bible was so foreign to me that when I started reading, I was immediately confused. I had just started reading the New Testament. I finished the first book of Matthew and Jesus had already died? I called my dad, almost embarrassed to ask him but said, "Dad, can you clarify something about the New Testament?" He said, "sure honey". I said, "I don't understand, I just finished Matthew and Jesus already died. What's the rest of the New Testament going to be about if Jesus already died and rose again?" My dad was silent for a few moments, "Dad, are you there?" I'm sure he was stunned at the lack of knowledge I as a believer had in the stories of the Bible.

"Honey, the next few stories are going to be the same story told from different points of views from other disciples." I started laughing hysterically, embarrassed but thankful he clarified that for me! How could I have forgotten that? I thanked my dad and kept on reading. To my surprise, the Bible was insightful, uplifting, and inspiring. Side note, I hated reading. I never liked it… not ever!! When I did try, I would automatically fall asleep. I kid you not, it felt like I would go straight into a coma! This time, for the first time in my life, reading was enjoyable. Not only enjoyable, but relaxing and motivating. It quickly became a priority to my daily routine. It changed everything. I felt God gave me a new heart and joy for reading. What I learned later through my reading and study time with God, was while reading through the Bible, it made me feel like I was hanging out with God, just getting to know Him and His story and I thought that was super cool.

The Devil Knows the Scripture

Through reading, I had also taken notice that the Devil knew the scripture. When Jesus fasted for 40 days and 40 nights in the desert, Satan went there to tempt Him. Mind you, Jesus was hungry, thirsty, and exhausted and this is when Satan attacks. When we're down and vulnerable. Satan knew the verse from Psalm 91:11-12.

"For he will command his angels concerning you to guard you in all your ways; they will lift you up in their hands, so that you will not strike your foot against a stone." - Psalm 91:11-12

In Matthew 4:6 he records Satan tempting Jesus saying,

> ***"If you are the Son of God," he said, "throw yourself down. For it is written: "'He will command his angels concerning you, and they will lift you up in their hands, so that you will not strike your foot against a stone."' - Matthew 4:6***

It was a great reminder that if the Devil knows God's word, I should know God's word. Satan can use anything against us, even scripture. He is like a wolf in sheep's clothing as Jesus says in Matthew 7:25.

> ***"Watch out for false prophets. They come to you in sheep's clothing, but inwardly they are ferocious wolves." - Matthew 7:25***

If we're not grounded in scripture, our defenses against the devils' schemes will be down and we will be easily deceived and easily misguided.

God Continues Speaking

After diving into the Bible and getting to know God better, He put in my heart it was time to go back to church. I really didn't feel like going to a church. I thought isn't this enough? It was not. God also added it's time to get baptized too. I never thought about getting baptized again. I mean, my parents baptized me when I was a baby, and I was a believer. He said, "You are being born again". When He put that in my heart, I almost started crying out loud. I would often sob during my runs just thinking about giving my heart and my life over to Christ because for the first time in my life, it was coming from the deepest part of my soul. It wasn't coming from the idea or the thought "I am a believer", "I am a Christian". No, it was because I was choosing Him, I needed Him, I wanted Him and Him alone.

> ***"Ask and it will be given to you; seek and you will find; knock and the door will be opened to you. For everyone who asks receives; the one who seeks finds; and to the one who knocks, the door will be opened." - Matthew 7:7-8***

Our Dependency on Christ

I then realized my lack of God and my need for God. If I had known then what I know now, I know my life would have been a very different reflection of peace, joy, and freedom. I believe most believers in Christ are true believers, but not true followers. It's a hard truth, but I can stand by this because that was me. Talking and believing I was a follower of Christ, but not walking the walk, I was a believer, not a follower. What does that mean? The true believer does believe in God, he has accepted Him and asked for God to be Lord over his life. Believes that God's son is Jesus, our Lord and Savior who died for our sins, believes in prayer, believes in the Bible (for the most part, maybe it's not all real but lessons), believes in Heaven… maybe Hell (why would God create Hell if he's all loving?), understands sin is a bad thing and yet it is within our flesh and nature. Believes forgiveness is important (for the most part, wait…can God really forgive me and do I really have to forgive everyone?) I would consider this a true believer but with lots of questions and doubt. One could say that these bombardments of thoughts are a combination of lack of confidence in God, our questioning if God is a good God, and the supernatural forces against us. Let's reflect…

- **Lack Of Confidence in God**

  We forget God Has Us, God Loves Us, and God Wants Us. The lack of confidence is not your disbelief in God. It's your uncertainty that He's there for you no matter what. It's also the inner conflict of putting the confidence in yourself verses God. This could be any kind of trauma we've been through - childhood trauma, to current day trauma. This could be our view of the world or our lives in the world, the pain, the suffering, the conflict, war, depression, disabilities, addictions, abandonment, loss, sickness, our sin, our imperfection, our unforgiveness. It's ongoing because, we do live in a fallen world, and we are fallen people. Ever feel like the weight of the world is on your shoulders? That's your dependency you carry on yourself. Why would you carry the weight of the world if God has already done that for you? God never intended for us to carry our burdens alone. That is why He sent His son Jesus. We are to lay our burdens down at the foot of the cross and trust God to handle the things that are too big for us. Even if we feel like we got it, we should put our confidence in God knowing he has our best interest at heart and that He knows us better than we know ourselves, because He made us! This is another way the devil gains a foothold on you. He wants you to believe that your burden is yours and yours alone. But scripture tells us differently! In Galatians 6:2 it reads, ***"Carry each other's burdens, and in this way you will fulfill the law of Christ."*** We can lay our burdens down and give them over to Christ as well as share our burdens with others, sharing not dumping! God made a world full of people so we could all be a part of each other's lives, it's a shared responsibility!

"For by the grace given me I say to every one of you: Do not think of yourself more highly than you ought, but rather think of yourself with sober judgment, in accordance with the faith God has distributed to each of you. For just as each of us has one body with many members, and these members do not all have the same function, so in Christ we, though many, form one body, and each member belongs to all the others."
- Romans 12:3-5

Confident, meaning - the feeling or belief that one can rely on something or someone: a firm trust. Trust that God has you no matter what your circumstance or situation is and that He also puts people in your life to help you share your burden. You are not meant to do it alone.

- Is God a Good God?

"Every good and perfect gift is from above, coming down from the Father of the heavenly lights, who does not change like shifting shadows."
- James 1:17

God never changes, even though our circumstances do. He is the same God, from the beginning of time until the end of time. If you're having a hard time with the idea God is all good, look at your life. Sometimes we feel God is picking on us, or that he has abandoned us, but that simply is not true. God challenges us at times and even isolates us to help us grow personally and to draw us back to Him. Also recognizing that the world is broken and what the devil does to disrupt or cause pain in our lives, God will use for our good.

"I have said these things to you, that in me you may have peace. In the world you will have tribulation. But take heart; I have overcome the world." - John 16:33

"And we know that for those who love God all things work together for good, for those who are called according to his purpose." - Romans 8:28

"As for you, you meant evil against me, but God meant it for good, to bring it about that many people should be kept alive, as they are today." - Genesis 50:20

REMINDER: WHAT THE DEVIL MEANT FOR BAD, GOD MEANT FOR GOOD

In this last verse, Genesis 50:20, this is an extraordinary story of one man's faithfulness, patience, grace, and forgiveness. Joseph was the most beloved by his father Jacob, who was given an impressive robe of many colors. His brothers were jealous, angry, and despised him. It didn't help that Joseph flaunted a little bit about his recent dream foreshadowing that his brothers, the moon, and the stars would one day bow down to him. One day his brothers decided to get rid of him, so they seized him and sold him into slavery to a party of Ishmaelites, or Midianites, who carried him off to Egypt. The brothers thought that would be the last of him, but God had different plans. Joseph no doubt had hard times, for 13 years he suffered and was even imprisoned. Eventually, Joseph gained favor from the Pharaoh of Egypt from his gift of interpreting his dream. He obtained a high place in Pharaoh's kingdom, appointed second only to the King himself. The significance of this was that he was able to save thousands of people not only in Egypt, but from outside areas when a huge disastrous famine hit. This was pharaoh's dream that God gifted Joseph to see. Not only was Joseph able to save thousands of lives by helping the Egyptians prepare for the famine, he was also able to save his brothers, his entire family, and was gifted with immense power and prestige for 80 years. This story has so much in it. I strongly encourage you to read the entire story to fully understand the power of God's love. God can use the wicked ways of our flesh for His purpose and our good. We all go through trials and tribulation, and we always will! We all experience pain, sorrow, suffering, abandonment, ultimately brokenness in some way. All our experiences are different, but the same. We all feel sad, lost, and broken at times and call out to God asking Him why? The above verses from the bible are great reminders that God is a good God, and a loving God. We don't have to understand why things happen the way they do. My "Why God" story was exactly that. When we start to accept that we live in a fallen world tainted by sin, we can have that inner peace, the peace that only God can give us, not the worldly peace, but the peace that goes beyond our own understanding. We must believe and trust that God will work it out for our good because He is a good God, who absolutely loves us and adores us. This will require us to seek Him with all our heart, with all our mind, and with all our soul. Trusting that God will work all things out for our good as in Romans 8:28...

"FOR THOSE WHO ARE CALLED ACCORDING TO HIS PURPOSE."

We must also remind ourselves daily that we are victorious because God is victorious. When God sent His son down as an offering for us, the blood that was shed by Jesus was to free us from the sin we could never escape from. It was then that God won victory over Satan, and since Jesus left us with his Holy Spirit which resides in every believer, that means we also have already won victory! If we remember that we are victorious in Christ, it's much easier to overcome fear and the battles we face on a day-to-day basis knowing we've already won! It might not always feel like victory in that moment, but hold fast and trust that God knows best. His timing is very different than ours. Believe He is a good God, and you will see that God works in our favor despite our situations and circumstances and that He will make good what the devil meant for bad.

FORCES AGAINST US

- The Flesh- Our Personal Sin
- Supernatural Sin- The Devil, Demons
- The World- A Fallen Structure

Without getting too deep into spiritual warfare, as there is so much to learn, here are just a few things, you as a believer should know!

Being on guard to fighting personal sin, the flesh, us being human, being awake, spiritually awake and putting on the full armor of God to protect us from Supernatural Sin -
The Devil, The World:

"The god of this age (Satan) has blinded the minds of unbelievers, so that they cannot see the light (the truth) of the gospel (God) that displays the glory of Christ (Jesus), who is the image of God (our savior)." - 2 Corinthians 4:4

"They are darkened in their understanding (shut out by God), alienated from the life of God because of the ignorance (lack of knowledge) that is in them, due to their hardness of heart (which comes from living in this world)."- Ephesians 4:18

PUTTING ON THE FULL ARMOR OF GOD

Side Note: My husband and I were so encouraged by this upcoming verse that we started a clothing company called ***Lord and Armor***. The idea behind it is simple: every time you wear one of our shirts, hats, or hoodies, it's a representation of putting on the armor of God. Little did we know, ***Lord and Armor*** would become more than just a clothing brand – it's becoming the cornerstone of all our businesses, all with the aim of drawing people closer to Christ.

"Put on the full armor of God, so that you can take your stand against the devil's schemes. For our struggle is not against flesh and blood, but against the rulers, against the authorities, against the powers of this dark world and against the spiritual forces of evil in the heavenly realms. Therefore put on the full armor of God, so that when the day of evil comes, you may be able to stand your ground, and after you have done everything, to stand. Stand firm then, with the belt of truth buckled around your waist, with the breastplate of righteousness in place, and with your feet fitted with the readiness that comes from the gospel of peace. In addition to all this, take up the shield of faith, with which you can extinguish all the flaming arrows of the evil one. Take the helmet of salvation and the sword of the Spirit, which is the word of God. And pray in the Spirit on all occasions with all kinds of prayers and requests. With this in mind, be alert and always keep on praying for all the Lord's people."
-Ephesians 6:11-18

(From the Life Application Study Bible:
New International Version)

Piece Of Armor - Use – Application

Belt: Truth

Satan fights with lies, and sometimes his lie sounds like the truth: but only believers have God's truth, which can defeat Satan's lies.

-This is why learning scripture is so important. The truth is God's word. Start reading your Bible, ground yourself in it, absorb your mind with His Word, so you may know the difference between God's voice and the Devils.

Breastplate: Righteousness

Satan wants us to think that telling others the Good News is a worthless and hopeless task- the size of the task is too big, and the negative responses are too much to handle. But the footgear God gives us is the motivation to continue to proclaim the true peace that is available in God –news everyone needs to hear.

- Satan will belittle every good thing God puts in your heart, including sharing your faith and your love for Christ. Don't be afraid, be bold, stand up for God and be the light for the dark world we live in.

Shield: Faith

What we see are Satan's attacks in the form of insults, setbacks, and temptations.
But the shield of faith protects us from Satan's flaming arrows. With God's perspective we can see beyond our circumstances and know that ultimate victory is ours.

- Don't focus on the storms, the negative things, or the hard things in your life. That is Satan using what he has to keep you from succeeding and following through with Gods plan for your life. You have Victory because Christ has already won. Take the authority Jesus has given you through the Holy Spirit and use it!

Helmet: Salvation

Satan wants to make us doubt God, Jesus, and our salvation. The helmet protects our minds from doubting God's saving work for us.

-Your thoughts are not always your own, protect your mind for the mind is where Satan attacks and the ripple effect of his will is disastrous. God died for you, you have been saved, reject Satan's voice in the name of Jesus. "I reject that thought, in the name of Jesus". Watch what happens!

"I REJECT THAT THOUGHT, IN THE NAME OF JESUS"

Sword: The Spirit, the Word of God

The sword is the only weapon of offense in the list of armor. There are times when we need to take the offensive against Satan. When we are tempted, we need to rest in the truth of God's Word.

-There's no better way to counteract Satan than with the Word of God. The name of Jesus is the most powerful name there is. Even demons flee when they hear His name. Claim the name of Jesus, speak it, and use it, it is your sword against the enemy. Being unaware, unguarded, or being ignorant makes us easy targets for a spiritual attack which can allow our minds and thoughts to go astray and down a rabbit hole of negative, bad, ungodly, not our own thoughts and even actions. Questioning God, believing in our own efforts over God's goes against everything one does to believe in, trust, and walk with God. I'd like to break down the next two chapters about the two different paths of the Christian belief. The believer not the seeker, and the believer who seeks.

To wear your armor you can find us at
www.lordandarmor.com and follow us on Instagram
@lordandarmor (click on QR Code below)

CHAPTER 2

The Believer Not the Seeker

CHAPTER 2
The Believer Not the Seeker

Sure, we all question God. We question Him on many different subjects such as our suffering, the world's suffering, evil, and even the silence or what feels like the absence of God. When we do this, there are three things that take place and start to take root in our foundation. We lack the confidence in God, we question if God is really a good God, and we forget about the supernatural battle we face daily whether knowing it or not. You're not alone! This is a natural and agreeable place to go especially in trying times. It's also a very human characteristic of our fallen nature to worry, to fear, and to question. Most people, even believers, have a hard time understanding the concept of God. What's the harm in questioning God or our faith? There is no harm for someone who lives their life outside of God, but for those of us who are seeking God and stating we believe in him, it's a very easy way to start becoming our own God. It's easy to replace God with almost anything and everything. Ourselves, our spouses, our children, our jobs, our hobbies, money, success, fame, our scrolling on social media, our favorite TV show, our favorite band, the list goes on! We all fall short of the glory of God; we all live and serve ourselves and replace God almost daily with our own interests and desires without even thinking. It's our humanness. It's our sin. If we plan on questioning God, then it should be our curiosity to know Him deeper, but much of the time it becomes more about ourselves than God. If we are true believers and followers of Christ, one of the most important things we can do is surrender to Him daily.

> ***"But seek first his kingdom and his righteousness, and all these things will be given to you as well."***
> ***- Matthew 6:33***

If we seek God first and surrender to him daily, we in return are dying to ourselves (our flesh, our sin) and we are putting God as priority over our lives.

> ***Then Jesus told his disciples, "If anyone would come after me, let him deny himself and take up his cross and follow me." - Matthew 16:24***

When we put our trust in Him instead of our own doing even our own understanding, God will make provision for us no matter what our situation or circumstances are. A lot of the time it won't add up or make sense in that moment, but that's for God to deal with and us to trust in. I love this verse in Deuteronomy...

"There are some things the LORD our God has kept secret, but there are some things he has let us know. These things belong to us and our children forever so that we will do everything in these teachings." - Deuteronomy 29:29

We are not meant to know everything, only God knows everything. It's not about understanding how it all works, it's about understanding our design and our image in Christ and our natural desire to draw into closer relationship with Him. Unbelievers and believers alike are all drawn to something bigger than themselves. However, we know, this is God's specific design to pull us closer to Him.

"And without faith it is impossible to please God, because anyone who comes to him must believe that he exists and that he rewards those who earnestly seek him." - Hebrews 11:6

If you're going to question the God you believe in, how is it that you truly have faith in Him? Our society has become a very "Self" society. Self-Care, Self-Help, Self-Love, Selfie. It's not about God or even others, it's about ourselves. As much as I love the idea of Self-Care and Self-Love, it should all be dependent on God, not ourselves.

"But when you ask, you must believe and not doubt, because the one who doubts is like a wave of the sea, blown and tossed by the wind. That person should not expect to receive anything from the Lord." - James 1:6-7

Maybe your doubt, your questioning, lack of faith and time with God is why you don't see him actively working in your life. Your shift of focus on your own plans verses God's plans for your life could be hindering and delaying the life and gifts God has in store for you and quite possibly already waiting for you. To unlock your blessings and gifts, you must simply believe and walk by faith. I say simply although we know it is not so simple. It's simple in the way we should go, we know the path that leads to everlasting life. Jesus is the only way! Believe in Him, accept Him as your Lord and Savior, walk by faith, and follow Him. However, living in this world and in our flesh, we are constantly bombarded with internal, spiritual, and mental attacks. There are three different ways we are constantly being influenced or attacked. First there is our number one enemy, the devil, second our flesh which is our humanness, and third the world, which became fallen and broken after Adam and Eve sinned. Each one of these work with the other but ultimately it is the devil influencing our flesh and the world, hardening our hearts, blocking out God and redirecting us back to ourselves and away from God.

The 1st Century Influencer

The word influencer is big these days, from TikTok, to Instagram, YouTube, Musicians, Celebrities etc... By definition an influencer is- *a person who is regarded as an expert within their particular field that also has a steady following. People trust their opinions, and thus their endorsements carry a considerable amount of weight. There is a growing interest in "experts" who have a large social influence and presence via social media.*

Heck, we can all be influencers today! How many people "follow" you? How many "followers" do you have? One thing I never thought about until I gave my life to Christ and decided to follow Him was the connection with social media and the self-absorption it can bring. Social media is a great tool in so many ways, but it's also a place where it can get you distracted and focused on you. How many times a day or how many hours a day do you find yourself scrolling or checking your Instagram, TikTok, etc? How excited do you get when you gain a new follower? How good does it feel when you see the number of "likes" and "views" your photo or videos get? I use social media too for all my businesses, so I already know your answer! Don't get me wrong, it's a great tool for marketing and advertising, but we have to be careful not to get self-absorbed or distracted. I'd like to talk to you a little about our very first influencer back in the 1st Century. Let's go back in time to the Garden of Eden where it all really started. One could say that the devil was the very first influencer at this time. He was an expert in sin and disobedience. He had many followers, the fallen angels that trusted him, believed him, and acted in rebellion with him. He is still influencing and holding us captive today with his demon army. People today still worship him, endorse him, and if they're not worshiping him, they're worshiping themselves or other outlets which is a win for him. That is his specialty and craft, influencing people to focus inward on themselves, worldly things, or other things that take the place of God. Since Adam was built from the ground up, in the likeness and image of God he was made perfect like God. He was sinless and so was Eve. They would often walk and talk with God in the Garden, and God's desire and intention was to teach them, and to know them. He wanted a personal relationship with them, a real, true, authentic relationship. God knew he had to give them free will for it to be real. One way he designed the Garden was that it had the Tree of Life or Tree of Knowledge in the center of the Garden. The one and the only rule God said to Adam was:

> ***"but you must not eat from the tree of the knowledge of good and evil, for when you eat from it you will certainly die." - Genesis 2:17***

This was a reminder to Adam and Eve that HE was God, and that their need was dependent on Him. It also allowed them free will and a choice, the same free will we have today. God wasn't saying they would immediately physically die. Although being exiled out of the Garden and into the fallen world it did bring about a physical death as we all still experience today. But what God was speaking of was a spiritual death. They would be totally separated from Him because God detests evil and cannot be in its presence. Unfortunately, Adam and Eve chose themselves over God. They allowed the devil to influence them. They listened to his lie, they thought about his lie, and then they acted on his lie despite knowing God's rule. They were deceived, disobedient, and it cost them their lives.

They both knew the choice that they made was against God, and when God asked them why they were hiding from Him they were filled with shame and blame. Adam blamed both Eve and God, and Eve blamed the serpent, but both knew it was their own doing. God was angry but He was and is a loving God, and He did not want to be eternally separated from his children. God being a good God, a God of mercy and love, was going to have to redirect his children as often parents must do when their children get out of line.

He used the exile or separation to bring his children, us as believers, back to him through repentance. And as we all know, He came down himself in the form of man to make right what we could never do on our own. This is so we could have the opportunity to have life in eternity with Him.

What is Sin?

What is sin? We can break it down a few ways according to Dr. Ed Murphy in the book "The Handbook for Spiritual Warfare". Although he applies this to the first introduction of Sin through Adam and Eve, we are an aftermath of their story.

1. Shame
2. Separation from God
3. Lack of Honesty before God
4. Blaming Others
5. Immediate judgment
6. Ongoing Spiritual Warfare

The Biblical Terminology of Sin or the broad terminology, within its biblical contexts, suggests that sin has three aspects:

- Disobedience to or breach of law
- Violation of relationships with people
- Rebellion against God (this is the most basic concept)

If Satan can attack in a place of pureness and paradise, surely he can attack in a broken and fallen world. Sin is within all of us, there's no escaping it since the fall of mankind. When Satan used the serpent to tempt Eve, it was first to question God and then to rebel against God. He's so subtle, so persuasive, sin is usually small, and can feel somewhat innocent. Pastor Dave (my pastor) mentioned that if God is not our daily focus and our daily priority, then our immaturity will weaken us in our faith and walk with Christ. This will allow Satan ground to tempt us in small ways which can add up to big ways!

> ***"Enter through the narrow gate; for the gate is wide and the way is broad that leads to destruction, and there are many who enter through it. For the gate is small and the way is narrow that leads to life, and there are few who find it." - Matthew 7:13-14***

There's only two paths, and yet so many small paths that lead away from God making the path pointing away from God a lot wider and easier to follow. Sin is more than just a choice...

> ***"Everyone who sins is a slave to sin". - John 8:34***

Sin arises from the heart, and it cannot be overlooked, it must be confronted and removed. Jesus came not only to teach of God's forgiveness, but to actually forgive and remove our sin Himself. The opportunity for forgiveness is given to all of us through Jesus. Sin separates us from God, it pulls us into our own lane, our own laws, our own beliefs, it rejects God and chooses self. Sin is not always an action, but many times simply a thought or desire. Repetitiveness of

"SIN REJECTS GOD AND CHOOSES SELF"

a bad habit, choice, or thought can lead many down the path away from God and as we all know, if we do one thing consistently enough it's easier to keep doing it whether it be good or bad. This is where we rationalize and justify our thoughts and our actions, replacing truth/God with ourselves/sin. Sin is ultimately the absences of God. It is a contagious parasite, it creates nothing, it feeds off of every good, beautiful, and true thing God ever intended for His children and His glory. So how do we turn away from sinning if sin is within us? We need to grow up, and mature in our walk with Christ. We need to draw closer to Him daily, surrender to Him daily, depend on Him daily. This will be a life long journey, but nonetheless a daily walk with Christ. Maturity in terms of a Greek word is translated as "perfect"but the meaning is "fully formed" or "brought to completion" which takes times. The standard for the Christian meaning of maturity is Jesus, and Jesus alone. Let's move forward to God working in our lives.

I Can Relate

I can relate with the lifestyle of a comfortable believer. I lived all of my life as a believer. I was raised in a Christian household. In fact, my father worked in the church for 45 years as the head Media Director at two of the biggest churches in Houston, Texas so I spent a lot of time and many hours growing up in the church. I always liked going to church and thought it was just part of life. I didn't know anything else! Every Sunday Dad would be out the door super early. Mom, my sister and I would get out the door just in time for the 11 a.m. contemporary service. We would stop at our local donut store, pick up some donuts, kolaches, and chocolate milk (gosh I miss those donuts and kolaches) and we would drive 30-45 minutes to church because we lived in Cypress, the suburbs of Houston. We would usually be on time, and a sweet older lady named Evelyn would save us seats in the very front row.

As my sister and I became teens, we would often sit in the back on the bleachers with a few other teens from our youth group, not paying too much attention but just enough. However, at the end of the service we would always receive communion with both mom and dad. Dad would come down just for that quick moment to take the bread of life (Jesus) and a sip of wine (His blood that was shed for our sins) and we would take in His remembrance together as a family.

I never stopped believing in God even in the hard times, but I also never had a real relationship with Him either. It's weird looking back and acknowledging I never sought Him, and I never chose Him to be priority and number one in my life. As I grew up and moved away, I really tried a few times throughout my life to go to church. I even joined a community group for some time, and I had started reading my Bible. I did search for Him after my mother died. I definitely had my "come to Jesus" moment and felt my need for Him, but I was still living for myself.

Test God, It's Okay

There was one Sunday I will never forget. I must have been 22 or 23 at the time and I was going on and off to a small church down the street. I had a $20 bill in my wallet, and I felt the Lord telling me to put it in the offering plate. I thought, "$20 dollars, you're crazy God!." Back then $20 for me was like having $100 or more. I NEEDED that $20 for groceries, gas, or just paying down some bills. I didn't have a lot of money although I worked my butt off and every little bit I had just went to the necessary things to keep me alive, or so I thought. I said to God, "If I put this $20 bill in the offering plate, I'm going to trust You to watch over me and provide for me. I'm not testing You, but I am!" There's a great Bible verse and it is the ONLY time we hear God say test me, and it had to do with an offering.

> ***"Bring the full tithe*** *into the storehouse, so that there may be food in my house, and* ***thus put me to the test****, says the Lord of hosts;* ***see if I will not open the windows of heaven for you and pour down for you an overflowing blessing."*** *- Malachi 3:10-12*

I trusted in Him enough to give the little bit that I had, and with that God did show up and He indeed blessed me. It was the first time in my life where I saw God working in ways that were not my own doing. At this time in my life, I was working at the Hollywood YMCA. I worked in almost every department you can think of. I was a Personal Trainer, A Fitness Instructor (Teaching Gravity Pilates, Indoor Cycling, and Yoga Barre). I worked as a Healthy Lifestyle Coach, I worked in the Membership Office, and I worked the Front Desk. At one time when they cut down my hours, I even worked in the Maintenance Department, and at other times I would pick up miscellaneous tasks from one of the managers (Ricardo Espinoza) that was kind enough to help me keep some hours so I could afford to eat and pay my bills. I was tired, exhausted, and still grieving from the loss of my mother.

During this time my health was also a mess. I had something called +4 Candida, which is something everyone has but when you have too much of it, it can make you feel like death. Candida is a yeast like parasitic fungus that can cause thrush and a slur of other issues. One of the more dominant symptoms I had was extreme fatigue and brain fog. At this time, I was unaware that my hormones were imbalanced due to high levels of stress from the loss of my mother. I believe that the Candida was another side effect from the amount of stress my body was under. Unknowingly I focused on fixing the Candida verses my hormones which offset my hormones more…but that's a story on its own! My health was suffering, and so was I. As I mentioned earlier that God had blessed me, He did. I was suddenly working with private training clients outside of the YMCA where I got paid double, sometimes triple the amount I was getting paid at the "Y". I was finally able to afford out of pocket services, to help get my health under control. At this time, I did not have health insurance because I couldn't afford it, and I've always come from the perspective of healing from the inside out, which meant I had to change my diet and my lifestyle quite a bit. All this cost money, money which I now had because of a simple "I trust you God". I kept giving and tithing every Sunday, and yes, I was giving 10% of my earnings as the good Lord asks. I was at the point where I was brining my check book to church and if I had missed a Sunday, I would double it. It felt good to give, and it also felt humbling to know that God cares, and he always provides. It's a lesson and a story I share often and am reminded of when times are financially tight, and it seems I'm not going to make it…yet every time I do.

Story Of My Life- Ground Hog Day

We really are like sheep. We stay on the path, and then at some point we get lost and go astray. This seemed to be the story of my life with my faith and relationship with God. I wanted it, I would try, but I never stuck with it. Why was it so hard? Looking back, my reasoning was usually, I'm too busy, I'll start reading the Bible next week, I'll start looking for a church, God knows I'm trying, I can't sit still, God forgive me, and repeat. In all of this I was always searching for my "purpose" and questioning "what am I doing here?" almost monthly! I'm not even kidding! It wasn't like I had a horrible life, and I was miserable with my life. I've been working for myself since I was 25 years old. I started my own Personal Training business in 2015, where I still train clients and offer Integrated Reflexology sessions. It's been a successful business and very freeing with flexible days and times for me to do other things. In 2021, I got my license as a Real Estate agent to help my husband in pursing his dream of opening his own Real Estate Brokerage where he does the mortgage side and I help him with the real estate side.

Again, I'm super grateful, we have a wonderful life, I have a wonderful life, but then why do I feel like I'm lost or still soul searching? This is where God steps in… if you allow Him. I was truly blinded by this world, and how I, let me emphasize "I" was going to accomplish all MY again "my" heart and mind wanted, although I couldn't even tell you exactly what that was, I just felt there was something bigger. I knew the life I had, and all my loss, pain, and experiences had been preparing me for something bigger than what I was doing, but what? I could tell you all the things I was passionate for - God, people, fitness, health, wellness, helping others, traveling, my family, but I was having a hard time understanding how they would or could all fit together to work as one. Realize the use of "I" as I'm soul searching for "myself". There's nothing wrong with having dreams, goal setting, or even planning ahead to some extent. My husband and I are go getters, we don't stop dreaming, and collaborating on ideas, ever! Our home is our home, workspace, creative space, thinking space, it's where we allow our minds to go wild! God really knew what he was doing when He brought us together. Most people call us a Power Couple and I believe that is very true.

We must remind ourselves daily, God's timing is not our timing, and we must surrender our ideal timeframe to Him because He knows best. When you say you need change or want change, consider that a nudge from God. He's encouraging you to take a leap of faith, to take some bold moves, be a risk taker, go with that crazy idea that's keeping you up late at night. How else can He work in your favor? But it's scary and so uncertain! More people than less, will stay with what becomes comfortably uncomfortable. In that case those who have chosen not to listen will complain daily. They will start to lack their confidence in God, and start to question Gods goodness. They will push through doing what they can leading up to a bitterness and discontent with their lives and with God. This is "Ground Hogs Day" as my mom would call it, the perpetual, continual, ongoing, walking zombie, small life Satan wants for us.

Satan is thrilled when we decide to shush God, live small, and live fearfully. He encourages it, and he knows it throws an anchor into God's amazing plans for our lives. Even as believers, we can become slaves to our sin allowing our minds, and spirits to be tortured and redirected by Satan. Remember, he is a cunning liar and will make you doubt yourself, your faith, your purpose, and ultimately God's goodness. Be strong in the Lord for He is faithful, and He is good. He truly loves you, cares for you, and wants the best for you. We will never be fully courageous without the guidance and accountability of God. He is the guy we want on our team!

Fear VS Faith

Replace fear with "the devil" and you can see that there is no use or need for fear in your life.

> ***"For God has not given us a spirit of fear but of power and of*** **love** ***and of a sound mind."* -**
> ***2 Timothy 1:7***

You know then, that if you're living and leading your life in fear, it is not coming from God. This includes the lack of confidence, not believing He is good all the time, and not putting on your spiritual armor to protect you against the things of this world and not of God. The problem with living your life in fear is that it prevents God from fulfilling His will for your life. It will hold you back from every good thing God has for you. If you are the kind of person who keeps saying, "I got it," you are missing out on God intervening, sometimes through people he places in your life and sometimes through your circumstances. Lacking the confidence in God, will keep you vulnerable and it will open the door for Satan to use fear as his tactic to keep you self-focused on your own tasks, win or lose, succeed, or fail.

FEAR IS A LIAR

Fear disguises itself in many different forms such as anxiety, worry, despair, and anger. When you allow fear in, more than likely it will stop you in your tracks. It will stop you from moving into any courageous ideas you have in your heart or in your mind. It will keep you focused on the worries of this world, the stresses of your family, your job, your finances. The despair, that voice in your head that says you're not good enough, it's a stupid idea, you'll never be able to amount to that. Maybe even anger the kind that drives you and motivates you but in return takes your eyes off the Lord and into a self-reflecting, self-seeking pain, where all the hurt, and all the suffering you've endured over the years has you asking "God, where are you, don't you care?". How can you have real faith when you are questioning if God is with you? You have replaced your faith with fear.

"It's a Ghost!"

Here's a great story to remember, to look to Jesus and not ourselves, not our circumstances, or even our own understanding. In the Bible Jesus had just preached and fed over 5,000 men. This doesn't include the women and children, so there were approximately 15,000-20,000 men, women, and children who witnessed the miracle that Jesus performed. He fed the entire hungry crowd from only five loaves of bread and two fish. There were even leftovers as it says in the Bible.

"YOU HAVE REPLACED YOUR FAITH WITH FEAR"

"Everyone ate until they were full. When they finished eating, the followers filled twelve baskets with the pieces of food that were not eaten."
- Matthew 14:20

After Jesus fed the crowd, He sent his disciples by boat to go to the other side of the lake. Jesus stayed behind to say his goodbyes to all who came to hear Him. He then retreated to the hills for his prayer time and quiet time with God His Father. If you know the story I'm about to talk about, then you'll see where I'm heading with this story. Going back to his disciples making their way to the other side of the lake by boat. There were very strong winds that morning creating huge waves, making it very difficult to get to the other side. Suddenly they saw a figure walking toward them on the water. Of course, we know this was Jesus, but they had their doubts.

"When they saw him walking on the water, it scared them. "It's a ghost!" they said, screaming in fear. But Jesus quickly spoke to them. He said, "Don't worry! It's me! Don't be afraid. Peter said, "Lord, if that is really you, tell me to come to you on the water." Jesus said, "Come, Peter". But while Peter was walking on the water, he saw the wind and the waves (he was focused on his fears instead of Jesus). He was afraid and began sinking into the water. He shouted, "Lord, save me!" Then Jesus caught Peter with his hand. He said, "Your faith is small. Why did you doubt?" - Matthew 14:26-31

Often our stories our very much like Peter's. We question if God is there, and then we shift our eyes onto our fears, our problems, our insecurities, our anxieties, our worries, our doubt, our despair, our anger instead of keeping our eyes focused on God and trusting Him. The opposite of fear is faith.

When you use your faith, you're fully trusting God even when your circumstances or your life feels against you. If you can just remember this...

FAITH IS CONFIDENCE

"If God is for us, who can be against us?"
- Romans 8:31

Another great reminder that God has already won victory and if He has won, so have we. Often times we say we have faith and trust in Him, only to find out we're standing in our own way. Faith cannot work unless we put it into action. If there's anything I've learned in my fitness career by physically pushing and training my mind and body, it is that it takes action. I can't just say I'm going to compete in a triathlon, train to place and then not practice. I must follow through and commit and take action. That might mean I have to get up extra early, change my diet, do two-a-day workouts and push myself daily to reach that long awaited goal. It will have to be something I surrender daily to in order to create that habit of consistency. If I want to get up on the podium and receive my medal, I will have to put my focus, my desire, and my goal into action. Faith is the same. It's just another muscle we must train. And let's be honest, faith doesn't happen overnight. It's going to take some practice and consistency. The human thing to do is trust ourselves more than others. Why would it be any different with God?

It's natural in our design, and with the fallen world we live in filled with broken and hurt people, it makes a lot of sense to trust ourselves more than others. One could say we are even conditioned for it! Some sayings we've heard throughout our lives are Dog Eat Dog, Survival of the fittest, it's a cut-throat world, can't trust nobody but yourself! It's sad, and often true, but God is very different. We cannot place God in the same box as we place ourselves or others. He is the source of life. If there's anyone you can trust and rely on, it's Him. Learning to lean on Him, trusting He is a good God, and having the faith to surrender to Him daily is going to take some practice. I always explain it this way to my clients, "When it comes to being consistent in building a healthier lifestyle, it's just like brushing your teeth. You don't even notice you're doing it, because you do it every day, it's just what you do!" I remember teaching my stepson at age four how to brush his teeth properly and having to tell him to do it every morning and every night, and of course don't eat or chew the toothbrush, brush with the toothbrush! I'm still reminding him and he's 14! Faith works the same way. It's a daily practice, the more you work that faith muscle, the easier it is to have the truest form of confidence in Jesus and truly walk by faith.

"So faith comes from hearing, and hearing through the word of Christ." - Romans 10:17

"And without faith it is impossible to please him, for whoever would draw near to God must believe that he exists and that he rewards those who seek him." - Hebrews 11:6

This will lead us into our next discussion…the believer who seeks.

CHAPTER 3
The Believer Who Seeks

CHAPTER 3
The Believer Who Seeks

"You will seek Me and find Me when you search for Me with all your heart." - Jeremiah 29:13

The seeking believer approaches faith with a hunger and thirst for an intimate relationship with God. It's different than just believing, and deeper than just saying, "I am a believer." Seeking God means searching for God. How do we find God? As the Bible verse above describes the only way to find God is to search for Him with all our hearts. How do we do this? It seems so simple, like a child playing Hide and Seek. You go hide, and I'll come find you. If you remember playing this game, sometimes it would get almost frustrating when you couldn't find the other person hiding. Like they disappeared or maybe they were cheating, and they kept moving around to the point you would just give up. We as Christians are kind of living in that place as children do in the game of Hide and Seek. Our seeking can get lost in our day to day lives and somewhere in our search, we stop and give up. We don't give up our belief, but we're also not living our lives searching for God. Finding God is a combination of growing deeper in love with Him, diving deeper into relationship and communion with him, and learning who He is through His word. A few questions for you…

Are you on a daily mission to know God more? Do you crave time with Him and act on it? Are your thoughts aligned with His thoughts? Do you take the time to be still with Him? Your entire heart must be searching to know Him better. The world is so easily distracting - our jobs, our lives, our families, all social media, the internet, TV, same things we talked about in the previous chapters. How do we get to a place where we put God first? There are 24 hours in a day. How do you prioritize your day? I know what you're thinking - if I add one more thing to my day I'll explode. I don't have enough hours in my day, in fact I need more. I'm just too tired at the end of the day. I used to say all the same things, and yes there's always truth to the busyness of our lives, but we're talking about time with our Creator, our Heavenly Father, our Savior! If we can't make time for Him, then what else matters? We must come to an understanding that this life is not the life we're living for! What? Mind blown, I'm alive and I feel very much like I'm living in this world. NO and YES. We live in this world, but we're not called to be of this world.

> ***"If the world hates you, keep in mind that it hated me first. If you belonged to the world, it would love you as its own. As it is, you do not belong to the world, but I have chosen you out of the world. That is why the world hates you." - John 15:18-19***

"Do not love the world or the things in the world. If anyone loves the world, the love of the Father is not in him." - 1 John 2:15

"Set your minds on things that are above, not on things that are on earth." - Colossians 3:2

We as believers should know that this world is not our home, this is not the end of the ride, and it is not our final destination. The life we're building here should be the life we're building for Heaven. It's definitely a hard thing to come to reality with on a day-to-day basis because we do have to live in this world. We still must eat, work, pay the bills, we have our God given desires to dream and achieve goals, we have families, friends, we have hobbies and interests. Life in this world is real too, and it is ever moving. Wrapping your head around the idea that this is all temporary can be overwhelming. So why are we here? What's our purpose? Our mission? Why did God even create earth?

"Roads? Where we're going we don't need roads." - Back to the Future, 1985

Every believer and non-believer has two paths. The first path is oneness with God and the second path is separation from God. These are both choices and each exists for both believers and non-believers. If you're currently living your life for yourself, you're choosing the path leading to separation (away) from God. If you're daily dying to yourself and surrendering your will to God, you are walking on the narrow path into unity and oneness with God. We as believers tend to go astray often as sheep do until we truly seek God with all our hearts. As I mentioned earlier, there is a daily surrender that must take place, or we will easily be tempted to fall back into old and bad behaviors that don't align with God's will for our lives. Our purpose on earth is to know God and love God. Our mission is loving others and redirecting those that have gone astray back toward Him for His glory and His Kingdom. God loves his children! When God created the world, heaven was in it, He was in it. He had no intention or desire of separating himself from us as we spoke about earlier in the book. He knew there was a risk by giving us a choice, but He was willing to take that risk so that there could be an absolute and true relationship with us.

Relationships

A relationship goes two ways! For my husband and me, I chose him, and he chose me. For our friendship, our love, and our relationship, we must choose daily how we speak to each other, how we listen to each other, how we work together, how we learn together, and how we grow together. These are all choices! Some days it's easy and other days it's hard.

WHEN GOD CREATED THE WORLD, HEAVEN WAS IN IT, HE WAS IN IT. HE HAD NO INTENTION OR DESIRE OF SEPARATING HIMSELF FROM US

We both make mistakes at times, we may argue, or disagree on a topic or point of view, we might say something hurtful, or put ourselves first instead of each other's needs, and parenting… it takes your relationship to a whole different level. There are choices every day on how we decide to speak, hear, and respond to one another. It is an ongoing life lesson! When you make the choice to stick it out and put the work in, it truly deepens your relationship and your intimacy with your spouse, making your lives as a whole, a whole lot easier! God desires that with us! He wants a deep and intimate relationship with each of us. He created us, He chose us, He loves us. The love He has for us is so big, we will never be able to fully understand how deep it goes because nobody on earth can love the way that God can. His love is perfect, and our love… is not. The neat thing is, he knows that!

He knew that to save us He was going to have to come down Himself in the form of man and sacrifice Himself so that we could be redeemed through Him. He knows we're not perfect, and with the free will He gave us, the risk was, we might not choose Him. Like Adam and Eve, we may choose ourselves which seems to be the often and preferred choice living in this world. As a believer, you're choosing Him as your life source. You're saying, I trust you, I believe in you, and I accept you as my Lord and Savior. You're choosing to have a relationship with Him because you hunger and thirst to know Him deeper. It's a commitment, it's something you'll be working on for the rest of your life just like a marriage. In fact, many times in the Bible it talks about Jesus being the bridegroom, and the bride being the church. There's a lot of weight on marriage for many different reasons, God is so specific in how he teaches us.

> ***"And Jesus said to them, "Can the wedding guests mourn as long as the bridegroom is with them? The days will come when the bridegroom is taken away from them, and then they will fast." - Matthew 9:15***

Jesus is talking about the day when he will die on the cross.

> ***Then I, John, saw the holy city, New Jerusalem, coming down out of heaven from God, prepared as a bride adorned for her husband" - Revelation 21:2***

This is the second coming of Jesus after the rapture. When God does a complete makeover of heaven and earth. This will be the place where God will dwell with all those who chose Him, His redeemed. There will be ultimate peace, light, and righteousness. It will be a city where there is no pain, no suffering, and no evil, it will be heaven on earth again. The other city is where the wicked will reside, and those who reject or did not choose Christ. It will be ultimate darkness, no light, no stars, no goodness, the complete separation from anything of good and light and of God. Hell is real, Heaven is real. Like a child having that little bit of fear in their father, it is good to fear God as it will keep us close to him.

Forgiveness

You must remember God is a forgiving God and a loving God. If you ask Him to forgive you, He will! One thing a true believer must do while asking for forgiveness is to then turn away from the sin he is asking forgiveness from. It's like when my kid acts out and does something wrong. I as his mother have a tense but loving conversation about his actions, we talk about it, and he says "I'm sorry." Naturally, I know he's not perfect and he needs to learn so I forgive him and say "great, let's move forward." But the next week, he does the same thing again! Now I'm a bit more furious. I speak to him in a loving but stern way. I may take something away that is important to him for punishment, and he apologizes. I say "okay buddy, let's try to make better choices" and of course I forgive him again because I love him. Well, three days later, he does the same thing again! I'm outraged, my son, my child, how could he do this to me? How can he keep saying he's sorry and then continue doing the very same thing he's not supposed to be doing? I go in this time, steam coming out of my head, tough love, and ground him!

He says he's sorry and he won't do it again. I then tell him that I don't believe him and that his sorry no longer holds any truth. I proceed in telling him he's not sorry, because if he was truly sorry, he wouldn't have done the same thing I asked him not to do again. My trust in him is now broken! My faith in him is blurred.

What does sorry mean to anybody if you keep doing the same wrong action and then apologize? Sorry won't mean anything until we truly turn away from our negative actions. It's very much like that with us and God. If you are truly asking for God's mercy and forgiveness from something you know does not align with God's will for your life and then you turn away from it, it is forgiven, it is done, it never existed! That's how powerful God's love and forgiveness are! In fact, I think there are over 67 Bible verses stating God's complete forgiveness for our sins, here are a few:

"I am he who blots out your transgressions for my own sake, and I will not remember your sins." - Isaiah 43:25

"For I will be merciful toward their iniquities, and I will remember their sins no more." - Hebrews 8:12

"And no longer shall each one teach his neighbor and each his brother, saying, 'Know the Lord,' for they shall all know me, from the least of them to the greatest, declares the Lord. For I will forgive their iniquity, and I will remember their sin no more." - Jeremiah 31:34

However, if you're going to continue doing the same things you know are not Godly and do not align with God and you do them without a care, why would God continue to forgive you? The question then is, are you truly a believer and a follower of Christ? Or are you ultimately living for God or yourself? Listen, our relationship with Jesus is not about us trying to be perfect and not make mistakes, because we will. It's not about us trying to clean up our lives before we accept Him and it's not about Jesus trying to clean up our old messy lives to then save us. It's all about us coming into a new relationship, and a new life with Jesus! By accepting Him, you have accepted a new life through Christ.

As a personal trainer to my clients, the same idea applies. You can't look at your unhealthy lifestyle and start cutting out all your bad habits all at once, it's not realistic. It's not about you getting into better shape first, only then to reach out for my help. Even with their diet, it's not about having a clean and perfect diet to then start working out. The ultimate goal is a healthy lifestyle change which is a commitment to a lifetime of taking care of yourself! That means that it must be organic, consistent, and then put into action.

Your relationship with taking better care of your body will be a gradual process, and I as a trainer salute anyone willing to come in when they're a mess and are willing to seek help and guidance. I don't judge them at all, I'm grateful they came to seek my counsel, and I do my best to show them the way. Accepting Jesus alone is not enough to be a true follower of Christ. It's a two-way relationship and it is a forever journey with Him. It doesn't end when you ask Him into your life, that's where it begins.

ACCEPTING JESUS ALONE IS NOT ENOUGH TO BE A TRUE FOLLOWER OF CHRIST. IT'S A TWO-WAY RELATIONSHIP AND IT IS A FOREVER JOURNEY WITH HIM. IT DOESN'T END WHEN YOU ASK HIM INTO YOUR LIFE, THAT'S WHERE IT BEGINS

God's Two Greatest Commandments

> **Jesus said*: 'Love the Lord your God with all your heart and with all your soul and with all your mind.' This is the first and greatest commandment. And the second is like it: 'Love your neighbor as yourself." - Matthew 22:36-40***

If we can uphold any of the 10 commandments, these are the two God favors the most. We are to love God with all of ourselves, all our hearts, all our minds, and all our souls! We are also called to love others because they too are image bearers of God, just like you and I, and God absolutely loves us all. Drawing closer in fellowship with others is just as important as drawing closer to God. If we want to find God and grow deeper in relationship with Him, we must be able to draw closer in deep relationship with people too. At times, I find it harder to love people more than to love God. Just like you and I, people are flawed. Our spouses, our children, our parents, our friends, our co-workers, mentors, and neighbors. There's no way around it, we are all out for ourselves and that's just the daily truth. God wants us to love others just as much as we love ourselves. You may not think much about loving yourself, but how many times a day do you think about what your needs or wants are? How often do you feel the urge to complain or vent about the things or people in your life that aren't fair? How about venting to God and telling Him what's up? Don't I deserve better? I know I do at times! Is that wrong? Not really, they are real feelings, but the problem is a lot of the time we get caught up in a spiral of negative thinking that could lead us down a path of bitterness, resentment, and anger towards God, and others. This is where Satan's deceitful tactics come in. He's got you right where he wants you and he's giving you a big thumbs up to keep going. He's your biggest fan, and he's cheering you on! You're starting to feel pretty confident in yourself about the unfairness that's being dealt to you. This is now the place where we give ourselves permission to blame God, blame others, question God, and decide to confide and trust in ourselves to get what we want, how we want it, when we want it. It's a self-righteous attitude where we justify everything. We feel we are deserving of more. Let me let you in on a little secret…none of us is deserving!

I'm Not Deserving, You're Not Deserving

I used to get caught up in the idea that I deserve, well a lot of things. I deserve happiness, I deserve love, I deserve things that work in my favor, I deserve a great life, I, I, I. The truth is none of us is deserving of anything. I could write a book of all the good things I've done in my life for others that would justify why my life should be so great and why I deserve more. However, Jesus never promises us an easy life. He basically said the opposite. Jesus said,

> **"I HAVE TOLD YOU THESE THINGS, SO THAT IN ME YOU MAY HAVE PEACE. IN THIS WORLD YOU WILL HAVE TROUBLE. BUT TAKE HEART! I HAVE OVERCOME THE WORLD." -JOHN 16:33**

He's letting us know right away that this world will not always be kind, we will struggle, and we will go through pain and discomfort. But He also says, take heart, meaning be confident, be courageous, because He has overcome the world, meaning, there is hope and we can trust in knowing our eternal life ahead will be one filled with the ultimate joy, peace, and love we so much crave here on earth. **If we allow our self-righteous attitudes to take the place of our faith and our trust in the Lord, we are headed down a path away from Christ and towards ourselves.** The question then becomes, how do we fully trust God when we're suffering? How do we love others as we love ourselves? How do we stay focused on Him when we're not happy with our lives?

Here are a few tips on how to love more like Jesus...

1. **Be Attentive-** be present and giving of your time with others. Don't just listen, HEAR what they have to say.

2. **Be Welcoming**- stop looking at your phone when you're walking around, put a smile on your face, and include others even if they differ in opinion, status, or walk of life.

3. **Be Gracious**- stop judging people and that includes yourself. Give yourself grace and give grace to others. People make mistakes, we all mess up, show a little kindness and forgiveness, it's what Jesus would do (W.W. J. D)- What Would Jesus Do?

4. **Be Fearless**- God has given us the spirit of power, love and, self-control so stop living in fear. Fear is a liar, don't be afraid to step out and meet people. God works through people. If you hold back, you'll be missing out on God's blessings for you, and the opportunity of blessing others.

5. **Be Giving** - We already invest a lot of time into ourselves, start investing your time in other people!

Ask For God's Help

The only way to ultimately trust God over ourselves, love Him whole heartedly, and love others as ourselves is to ask God to help us. We need His help! We cannot do it alone. It is too big, and too much for any of us to get through the hardships of life without Him. You can be the kindest person in the world, but you're still going to make mistakes. You can have a great life, and still go through hard times and moments of doubt. We've all had people hurt us, abandon us, lie to us, and betray us. How can we truly love and forgive our enemies and those who have hurt us? We cannot do it alone; we can only do it with God's help. Psalms 41:6 *"God is our refuge and strength"* We must rely on His strength over our own. I remember praying to God asking Him to help me turn my life over to Him because I knew I couldn't do it on my own. I had tried so many times, and never was successful, on my own. It was only when I asked Him for help, that he showed up in a mighty way. My life has been changed forever since the day I asked Him to help me find Him and know Him. I now understand the power of prayer, and the power of asking the Lord for help. To rely on Him instead of my own efforts, to trust in Him, instead of myself, to walk by faith and not by fear, to know my life is precious to Him and that he's always with me. Whether I go astray, sin, or yell at Him, he's always with me.

God said, "Be strong and courageous. Do not be afraid; do not be discouraged, for the Lord your God will be with you wherever you go." - Joshua 1:9

"Even though I walk through the darkest valley, I will fear no evil, for you are with me; your rod and your staff, they comfort me." - Psalm 23:4

Even If…

There's a great song I heard on my run today and I wanted to share it with you as a reminder that God is a good and faithful God. That he loves you and wants to know you. To remember, that even if, life gets hard, and it doesn't seem fair instead of letting the devil get a foothold on you and allowing him to applaud your self-righteous and bitter feelings, find a way to praise God and thank Him. Thank Him for the life he has given you and for the eternal life you will have with Him because He saved you. We are triumphant, and we have victory, because Jesus has already won. When Jesus died on the cross for all of humanity's sins, it freed us from the sinful life we could never escape from. It allows us grace, acceptance, and forgiveness. Take that Satan! That is Victory! By the Holy Spirit we are cleansed of our sins, and we have an eternal place to rest when this world is over. This we can have hope in knowing, one day we will no longer feel pain, we will no longer suffer, and that we will be reunited with our Heavenly Father who created us, wants us, and loves us. **Turn your complaining into Praise and see how God will bless you and use you!**

"***Hallelujah Anyway***" by Matt Maher and Rend Collective

Scan the QR code above to listen to the song "Hallelujah Anyway"! It's been my go to as a daily reminder that even if things in your life feel out of control and you're in a hard place, find a way to praise God anyway! He will bless you for it, whether it's immediate or your eternal home awaiting, there are better days to come.

We're All the Same

If you want to know someone better, you spend time with them, right? You make it a priority to take time out of your day to come together talk, listen, and share. So how do we get to know God better aside from praying, asking God for help, asking for forgiveness, turning away from our sins, and loving others? He left us a timeless book, The Bible.

> **"Jesus said, "If you hold to my teaching, you are really my disciples. Then you will know the truth, and the truth will set you free."**
> **- John 8:31-32**

The truth is The Word, and The Word is God, the Bible exists only because of Him. He has left us with timeless truths and stories to know Him better. When you start reading the Bible you'll soon realize, people are the same today as they were at the beginning of time. There's a little relief knowing you're not alone on your faith journey. Many of the great leaders in the Bible had hardened hearts, were selfish, stubborn, and out of line. Here are a few:

Moses- Was a murderer and fugitive. He was also "slow of speech and tongue". He doubted that he was the right man for the job and even questioned God, BUT GOD chose him. We learn here that it doesn't matter how we view ourselves, or how lost we've become, God knows our hearts, and we will always have a choice to follow Him.

Saul (Paul)- Was a passionate persecutor of Christians. God revealed himself to Saul, Saul changed his name to Paul and became one of the most influential apostles, spreading the gospel and word of God throughout the world. We learn here that God can pick whoever He wants to lead people to Him. Sometimes it's a bad person, or a person who hates God and God's people, but God and only God can soften their heart and make the way for a transformation through His grace and forgiveness.

David- Was an adulterer and murderer. He was a man after God's heart, but he committed adultery with Beersheba and had her husband killed. When David was confronted by the prophet Nathan, he repented and turned away from his sins and wrote many of the Psalms which talk about repentance and forgiveness. We learn here that even when you're a faithful servant to God, you can still make mistakes, but God is a loving God and he's full of mercy and forgiveness.

Jonah- Was disobedient. God had told Jonah to go preach in the city of Nineveh. At the time Nineveh was perhaps the largest city in the world, about a three-day walk and it was filled with evil, wicked people. Jonah told God no and ran from Him. Naturally, because God can do anything and in my household we always say God has a sense of humor, He had him swallowed up by a fish. After three days in the belly of a fish, Jonah repented (I would too!) the fish spit him out, and he went and did as God commanded him to do. We learn here that God will redirect us when we go astray and when God tells you to do something, you better do it because he's going to get His way one way or another! Being obedient to God will open doors you never thought could open, He is the way!

The important thing to remember about these leaders is they were all flawed in some way. Just like us, their hard hearts were changed, and so can ours.

The world we live in can harden our hearts and disguise our true need for God into a true need for self. Every time we sin knowingly, our hearts become hardened causing a ripple effect of sinning. It's easy to get lost in the busyness of our lives, this world, and ourselves, but when we're focused on God and growing closer to Him, His truth is the compass that helps navigate us through life and to life. The Bible is his way of keeping us close to Him, and Him to us. Seeking God is seeking His Word. Spending time in the Bible will reveal God in ways you never knew Him. Learning the story of Jesus will bring you to your knees, the pure love and kindness of who He is will make you crave a new life in Him. A life that ultimately is transformed by His grace, and the power of the Holy Spirit.

THE WORLD WE LIVE IN CAN HARDEN
OUR HEARTS AND DISGUISE OUR TRUE
NEED FOR GOD
INTO A TRUE NEED FOR SELF

Be the Light in the Dark

I believe I was given the spiritual gift of Encouragement and Discernment. Spiritual Encouragement is the gift of encouraging and motivating others toward spiritual growth and maturity. Discernment of Spirits is distinguishing between different spirits, discerning whether they are of God, human, or evil origin. In Acts 1:8 it says: "But you will receive power when the Holy Spirit comes on you". All believers have spiritual gifts. It's an intimate part of you that's connected with God and His Holy Spirit. The moment you accept Jesus as your Lord and Savior, the Holy Spirit will come upon you and by His grace and divine empowerment certain spiritual gifts are bestowed upon you. They are not gifts for natural talents or skills, but rather to fulfill God's mission and serving others.

As I look back at many moments in my life, I've always had random people walk up to me and share their most intimate life stories with me. Sometimes it's in the first few minutes of meeting them, and others it's after a few times crossing paths. I've held strangers crying, I've hugged and prayed over others who were hurting or suffering. I've listened to Acountless stories of people who were lost or broken or just needed someone to talk to. For years I didn't understand why. Why me? I remember telling my dad at one point all my different stories of meeting people and connecting with them on such deep levels within minutes and just the feeling of confusion as to why. He told me, "It's because you have the light within, and people are attracted to the light…the light is Jesus."

Understanding that I have the light within changed my outlook and perspective on the world in many ways. I understood then that the world is dark and a lot of people feel hopeless. It's pretty interesting how much we all depend on light as a source to sight. In the darkness, it feels uncertain, scary, unknown, and ultimately hopeless. Have you ever lit a single match in a dark room and then have that feeling of hope and relief? It's quite amazing how much light can come from one little match. We are that little match! God's light is sufficient enough, His truth is sufficient enough, and His grace, love, and mercy are sufficient enough. We are called to be the light in this dark world. Representatives of Christ ready to love and serve others for His Kingdom and His Glory.

Speaking of being a light for others, another spiritual gift is The Spirit of Evangelism. Evangelists are those who proclaim the gospel and lead others to faith in Christ. This, I would say, is a new Spiritual Gift God has given me after surrendering my life over to him a few years ago and being born again. Recently, I had the honor of baptizing my sister and I also got to watch my husband baptize her husband. It was a beautiful moment, one I will never forget! My sister was a believer, but wasn't truly following Jesus, very much like my story and she wanted to recommit her life completely back to Him. Her husband, Chris had recently accepted Jesus as his Lord and Savior but had never been baptized. We had planned a trip to St. Marteen months back, but it was the perfect place to baptize them both in the beautiful blue water in the Caribbean. I share this story as a testament as to why the light matters. My sister knows me better than almost anyone. She said she had been amazed to see such a change in me and also my husband, our relationship as a couple, my family, and my entrepreneurial adventures. She saw God working, and she wanted that too! God can use anyone to draw them closer to Him. Whatever your Spiritual Gifts are, use them and be a light in this dark world. The world so desperately needs Jesus! We as Christ followers get to be a part of bringing His Hope and His light to the lost and the broken. If God can meet us where we are, we should be able to do the same for others.

A Little Bit of Poop

This is a classic and timeless story, thanks to my mother. I wish I could ask her the exact reason why she shared this story in this particular fashion, and if this was something she came up with on her own, but I'll have to do my best to remember. Rachel and I must have either A.) done something wrong or B.) wanted to watch a movie my parents disapproved of. I'm going to go with B as my parents were very strict on the things we were allowed to watch. Rachel and I would complain often about not being allowed to watch certain shows and movies.

IF GOD CAN MEET US WHERE WE ARE, WE SHOULD BE ABLE TO DO THE SAME FOR OTHERS

We'd say, "Why mom? All our friends have watched it, why can't we? Why do all our friends get to do things and watch things we can't?" This is a hard lesson for children that grow up with parents that are believers in Christ. It's hard to explain to your children the things of this world because honesty they just don't get it, and why would they? Most adults and people in this world don't get it! I didn't even get it until I fully turned my life over to Christ. It's not that we were bad kids who got into trouble all the time. It's the simple fact that what you see, and what you hear can influence you even if it's not in the moment. Once we normalize anything from violence, bad language, sex outside of marriage, witchcraft, that's it, we've accepted it, it is what it is, and it's not a big deal. However, our eyes, and our ears are portals to our soul. Of course it matters, and now I understand why my parents were so sensitive to having us partake in worldly films and TV shows. Well, Mom explains it this way. "If I gave you a brownie with a little bit of poop in it, would you eat it?" Rachel and I start laughing and ask her, "Well…how much poop?" She said, "just a little bit". We both look at each other agreeing, grinning, yet serious and say, "Probably". I'd like to say I take back the probably and say absolutely not, but this was the younger me! My mother proceeds, "Okay, so it's just a little bit of poop. But what if you eat that one brownie with a little bit of poop in it once a week? At some point even though it's just one brownie with a little bit of poop by the end of the month, you've eaten a big pile of poop! Do you want to eat a big pile of poop?" At that point we understood what she was trying to teach us. We didn't like hearing it, but she was right. A little bit of something not good, can add up and ultimately make a negative and long-lasting impact. It's best not to invite or even taste a little bit of evil, because I promise you, Satan will keep showing up if you let him and you won't even notice. He will disguise himself and bring ungodly things into your mind, your heart, and your soul. He will normalize the evil, and you will justify that it's no big deal. If you give him a little bit for long enough, he will use what he gets to bring you down. His plan for your life is only death and destruction, and it can start with just a little bit of poop.

I'm a CHRISTian

I have so many friends that are non-believers primarily because they don't like the way the Church and the people of the Church are, and I completely agree and understand. It's so sad to see people turning away from Christ because the Church and the people in the Church don't live like representatives of Christ. To call yourself a Christian, and a believer in Christ is more than just a saying. To be a true follower of Jesus and to call yourself a Christian you are saying, "I believe that Jesus is my Lord and Savior, I commit my life over to Him, and I strive to be more like Jesus".

Let's look at some of the qualities of Jesus, and I promise you it will be a lot longer than the 10 Commandments:

Qualities Of Jesus

> "Alertness, Attentiveness, Availability, Boldness, Cautiousness, Compassion, Contentment, Creativity, Decisiveness, Deference, Dependability, Diligence, Discernment, Discretion, Endurance, Enthusiasm, Faith, Flexibility, Forgiveness, Generosity, Gentleness, Gratefulness, Hospitality, Humility, Initiative, Joyfulness, Justice, Love, Loyalty, Meekness, Obedience, Orderliness, Patience, Persuasiveness, Punctuality, Resourcefulness, Responsibility, Respect, Security, Self-control, Sensitivity, Sincerity, Thriftiness, Thoroughness, Tolerance, Truthfulness, Wisdom, Virtue." - from Christway Counseling Center (website listed in references, page 150)

When you can aspire to these qualities like Jesus, then it is fair to say you are a Christian. I didn't say a believer, but a true follower and representative of Christ. To **represent** means *to be appointed to* ***act or speak for (someone)***. That holds a lot of weight and yet we throw around the idea that we are Christians even when we continue living in a way that goes against who Jesus is and who He's calling us to be. No wonder people are pulling away from the Church, and criticizing the people in the church. Satan works hard in the Church, no doubt about it. It's a great place to stir up some self-righteousness, and hatred. If we are called to love others, then there is no place for pointing fingers at anyone but ourselves. When my stepson was little and he'd point his finger at someone else to find blame I'd say, "look at all those fingers pointing back at you!" He didn't like when I would say that, but it was the truth. We are only responsible for our own actions, not others. We don't have to agree but we can learn to love those who differ in opinion, politics, religion, sexual orientation, parenting, and so much more with God's help and only with God's help. It's not always easy but through Him it is possible. No need to be self-righteous when we are daily sinners, and all of us fall short of the glory of God. If we are to be true reflections of Christ, then let us love like Christ did. Remember, Jesus broke bread with tax collectors and sinners! Through our actions of love, we will reflect Christ, and God will work through us in other people. God can accomplish all His purposes without any help from us, but He chooses to work through us because it is good for us and a reminder, we cannot accomplish anything on our own. We cannot disrupt God's plans even if we tried, like I said earlier, God is going to get his way one way or another!

One Way or Another

Here's a personal story about being obedient and God having His way one way or another. When I started my faith journey with God, I slowly began to hear Him. It was more clear than ever before, and I knew it was Him. This only happened once I was fully committed to spending time with Him, spending time in prayer and in His Word. Often, I would pray before or after my study and I knew he had been working in my heart and changing it. I just felt different, a feeling of freedom, peace, and joy. Even when times were tough, there was this sense of true peace. The first time I heard God as I mentioned before was when He had told me to start reading the Bible, so I did. Then he told me to find a church and start going regularly, which I did. Then He told me to get baptized, which I did. I was being obedient to what He was asking of me, knowing, and trusting that He was now Lord over my life, and I was not. Listening to that quiet small voice and then moving into action shows God you are ready to do more for Him. When you start doing God's will, he will continue bringing more and then bigger opportunities your way. Sure, you can look at it as a test, but how else can God truly work in your life if you're not willing to listen and then take action? Here's an example! One day, I went out for one of my 30- mile bike rides and halfway through my ride I heard Him clear as day, I thought I was going to fall right off my bike! He said, "It's time to start your non-profit". It hit me so hard that without even thinking I responded back right away like He was riding right next to me. I said, "Yea, that sounds great" as I laughed, smiled, and deep down questioned. Side note, this non-profit idea had been on my heart since my mother died from breast cancer, going on 14 years now. He said, "it's time", I responded as usual, "okay, but how? I don't even

LISTENING TO THAT QUIET SMALL VOICE AND THEN MOVING INTO ACTION SHOWS GOD YOU ARE READY TO DO MORE FOR HIM know where to start." This is where it hit me in a way I'll never forget. He told me to reach out to a woman named Dana-Sue Crews. Okay, he now got my attention! "Dana-Sue, what does she have to do with my non-profit?" God said, "just reach out to her" and that was it. Just so you all know, Dana-Sue was a friend of my mother's. I had met her a handful of times back when my mom and her, and her husband Bill use to fundraise and race together for TNT. A few years later after my mother had passed, she put on a fundraiser event in honor of my mother for Team In Training. Outside of that, I think I ran into her randomly in Napa, California thanks to Facebook and that was it. I didn't know her life story, I didn't know anything about her other than she used to train, run, and fundraise with my mother. Back to my ride! I rode my bike home so fast, ran into the house with enthusiasm and a motive, and I told my husband, "Honey, God told me to start my nonprofit and he also told me to reach out to Dana-Sue, "Mom's friend". You should have seen the look on his face, it was priceless. His eyes were wide, and he just stared at me, confused and maybe a little concerned. Before he could say much, I of course had to call my twin sister Rachel to let her know we were doing this. This was our idea from over a decade ago and it was time. My sister picks up on the first ring and I tell her exactly what I told my Husband. "God told me to start the nonprofit and he also told me to reach out to Dana-Sue,"Mom's friend" are you in?" She was trying to get me to slow down so she could process my words as I kept talking,

"I have to do this, God asked this of me, I'm doing this with or without you, want to do it with me?" She slowly said, "Yes" and then asked me, "why Dana-Sue?" I replied, "I have no idea, but God told me to contact her." Just after hanging up with Rachel, I reached out to Dana-Sue through Facebook messenger, as I did not have her phone number. This is the exact message I wrote: "Hi Dana, I have a question for you about a fundraising idea. I thought maybe you'd be a good person to talk to about it. Do you have time this weekend to talk?" Dana Wrote: "I have some time tomorrow. And this will be great because I was going to wait a couple of weeks and reach out to you because I have an idea, I want to throw at you about you possibly writing a book. So, call me when you have time at (phone number)." Here is the One Way or Another, and God will have his Way! Even if I wasn't obedient, He was going to have Dana-Sue reach out anyway. What if I ignored God speaking to me or brushed it off? What if I thought it was a stupid idea, or it just wasn't possible! I've heard those voices in my head before, every time I would talk passionately about the idea of the nonprofit, Satan would win. Not this time! I had the armor of the Lord on and I was prepared for battle!

The intimate time I had been spending with God had softened my heart, opened my eyes, and opened my ears. I heard God clearly and it was glorious. A few days later, Rachel and I phoned Dana-Sue, and we pitched her our idea of the nonprofit that would help both cancer patients and their families, as well as those who were seeking a healthier lifestyle. She loved the idea and mentioned that she and her husband had their own nonprofit. That was it! I guess this is why God placed her name in my heart. She said she would be more than happy to walk us through the steps of getting ours started. She even said we could use her Articles of Incorporation that were written up from her lawyers from her nonprofit and go ahead and just replace their name with ours. By the time we had this conversation to the time we were approved by the IRS it was only three months! As I'm writing this book now, we had two fundraisers at the beginning of the year for a family in need and were able to raise just about $10,000 for them which was our goal. Isn't God good!

Our Mission: The Stride Project is a nonprofit organization dedicated to enhancing the quality of life for cancer patients and their families through a combination of fundraising and fitness challenges. The financial resources raised are directed towards sponsored families who have shared their stories with us. These funds are allocated to address their unique and pressing needs during this transformative and challenging period.

To find out more or be a part of our nonprofit visit www.thestrideproject.org or listen to our podcast at www.thestrideproject.podbean.com (we're also on Spotify and Apple)

Scan the QR codes below to see our website or podcast:

Your Timing is Not God's Timing

We often forget that we are not in control of life's situations and circumstances and its genius way of unfolding. Sometimes it works in our favor, and other times we are confused and frustrated feeling the odds are against us, or really that God is against us. God's timeline is different than our own. In Ecclesiastes 3:1 it says *"There is a time for everything, and a season for every activity under the heavens"*. God works all things in His perfect timing for our good, despite the evil and hardships that come with living in this world, Gods timing is never to doubt. If He is all knowing, and all good, then the best we can do is rest in knowing we are on the right path by surrendering our day and our lives to Him. If we are focused on ourselves, then we will feel the impact of the disappointment more. We will not be able to hold strong in knowing God is with us and He is for us. We will be like Peter, walking on the water but sinking because of the doubt in the hard times. Don't ever take your eyes off Jesus, you will surely drown in your fears, your insecurities, your doubts, and your failures. Your dependency cannot be in yourself, it must be in God. You have no control over the weather, just as much as you don't have control over your day to day. There's an old Yiddish proverb, "We plan, God laughs" this expresses the true reality of our human thoughts verses God's truth. We plan for things to go according to our planner, our calendar, our schedule, but many of times they don't. There is a quote with similar meaning by Woody Allen, "if you want to make God laugh, tell Him about your plans." We are only in control of how we manage our emotions throughout our day to day and that's hard enough. God is infinite, and we are not. God has great plans for each of us, even when we feel excluded, abandoned, or in a never ending darkness. Pslam 31:15 *"My times are in your hands"* Growing up or "Adulting" in your spiritual walk and faith will constantly be tested, not always by God, but sometimes. Allowing His timeline to take precedence over yours will show God you are ready for more. Character is built by overcoming trials and tribulation, not by having an easy way out. You were made for more than what you'll ever be able to give yourself credit for, just know that it is through trying times, missed appointments, unexpected delays that God comes into play. Be consistent in your faith, so you can be consistent with Gods timeline even if it doest' work out the way you initially planned.

BE CONSISTENT IN YOUR FAITH, SO YOU CAN BE CONSISTENT WITH GODS TIMELINE EVEN IF IT DOEST WORK OUT THE WAY YOU INITIALLY PLANNED

Give and Watch God Work

> **"Give, and it will be given to you. A good measure, pressed down, shaken together and running over, will be poured into your lap. For with the measure you use, it will be measured to you."- Luke 6:36**

Another way to draw closer to the Lord is through giving. Are you naturally more of a giver or a taker? Harsh sounding, but there are just as many takers if not more than givers in the world. If you really think about it, are you truly giving of your time? To God, your spouse, your children, friends or even strangers in need? Are you giving with your profits, what you make? Are you giving with your patience, your love, your encouragement, your forgiveness? These are qualities of Jesus and again, if we strive to be more Christ like, than these are the qualities we should be striving for as well. I'm not saying it's selfish to receive gifts and offerings, I love receiving gifts! But how much better does it feel to give than to receive?

When I was a teenager, I loved making gifts for my parents. I loved getting creative and making something thoughtful for them, something I knew would be special to them because it truly came from my heart. There are a few memories that come to mind. One time Rachel and I planned an Easter Egg hunt for Mom and Dad around the house. We thought it would be fun for them to run around

CHARACTER IS BUILT BY OVERCOMING TRIALS AND TRIBULATION, NOT BY HAVING AN EASY WAY OUT like kids again. We told mom and dad they each had 10 eggs hiding, and that once they found their 10 eggs they were done and had to wait 'til the other one found all their eggs. It was hilarious watching my mom run around like a crazy lady trying to find all her eggs. If you haven't figured it out by now, my mother had a very competitive spirit, even games were considered a competition and she wanted to win! I thought we had hidden our eggs pretty good, but she found them within minutes and started jumping up and down, giddy like a little child. Dad rolled his eyes because he had only found a few. Then Mom started pointing and shouting at the eggs she saw to help him, "Will over there, there's an egg, and oh there's another one". Dad looked at her and said, "I can find my own eggs, Susie!". We were laughing hysterically, telling Mom to let Dad find the rest of his eggs on his own.

It brought a lot of joy and laughter to both Mom and Dad, but especially to Rachel and me. The other fun memory was during Christmas time. I thought it would be fun to let both our parents open a really big present, that is one that was never ending! I found the smallest boxes all the way to the biggest box and wrapped each one, and yes it took forever, that's love! As soon as they opened the first big box, there was another, and then another, and another. This went on for some time, and they were cracking up. When they finally reached the end, there were two very tiny boxes wrapped, one for each of them.

When they opened their individual tiny box there was a note to each simply saying, "We love you". Once again, they enjoyed their time and their gifts, but most of all Rachel and I were filled with joy. Another story that fills my heart, was every Sunday on our way to church there was an older man named Curtis that used to sell newspapers under the bridge. Remember those? They're usually black and white, they have news stories, feature articles, advertisements, and correspondence, and they're pretty big. My mom would always pack Curtis a lunch and buy three to five newspapers from him even though we didn't need that many. We would all have a five-minute conversation with him, just checking in and seeing how he was doing. He always had the biggest smile on his face when we showed up. It was always a good feeling walking away from Curtis knowing we were able to give him a lunch, some money for the newspapers, and some company. This went on for a few years, then one Sunday when we went to get our Sunday newspaper, he was gone. I'll always remember Curtis and my mother's generous heart. There is truly something amazing that happens when you give with a cheerful heart. It's like God gives you an extra breath of life, you are filled with His peace, and there's a lightness that comes over you. So, what else does giving do that brings you closer to God?

1. It Deepens your Relationship with Him: Matthew 6:21 says, ***"For where your treasure is, there your heart will be also."*** When you give your time to God and give your time to others, you are drawing closer to God. If

God is our source of life, and our treasure, then that would mean the people He created in His image are His treasure. We can rest in knowing giving time and love to others will help us draw into closer relationship with Him.

2. It Molds your Character: If we are to follow in Christ's footsteps and conform to the image of Jesus, (not to the pattern of this world) then we know we can uproot our selfish hearts and replace it with a selfless heart. Jesus was not selfish with his giving, He always had time for every believer and non-believer. Growing closer to God and knowing Him to the deep level we desire comes with first building our character to reflect His image as talked about with the qualities that describe Jesus's character.

3. It creates Eternal Abundance in Heaven: Matthew 6:10-20 reads, ***"Do not store up for yourselves treasures on earth, where moths and vermin destroy, and where thieves break in and steal. But store up for yourselves treasures in heaven, where moths and vermin do not destroy, and where thieves do not break in and steal."*** 1 John 2:17 ***"The world and its desires pass away, but whoever does the will of God lives forever."*** This world is temporary, reading the Bible and spending time with God will be a daily reminder of this. It's so easy to forget the eternal life we should be living for, as we

wake up and move into our earthly day, and all the things that come with it. Our treasure is in Heaven with God. The more we can focus on spreading His word, loving Him, and loving others, we will receive our rewards and riches in our final world to come. I like new things just as much as anyone else, but our focus should not be on possessions of this world as much as it is as gaining our possessions in Heaven.

4. It Increases Your Abundance on the Earth - Proverbs 11:24-25: ***"There is one who scatters, and yet increases all the more, and there is one who withholds what is justly due, and yet it results only in want. The generous man will be prosperous, and he who waters will himself be watered."*** We can rest in knowing God wants us to be prosperous here on earth too. Generosity begets generosity…meaning it is contagious! If we give from the understanding that all that we are, and all that we have, is not truly ours or our own doing, then it stands on its own that giving and being generous is an advancement for the Kingdom and the Glory of God. God will bless you in this life, and the next when you bless others. Proverbs 11:25 ***"A generous person will prosper; whoever refreshes others will be refreshed."***

Just remember that when you're blessing others, you will feel the effect of that blessing just as much if not more. The more you give, the easier it is to continue giving. It's just like everything else we've been talking about in growing deeper in our walk with Christ. It's a muscle, and it needs to be worked! The more you work it, the stronger it gets, and eventually it will be as organic and natural as it is to breath.

CHAPTER 4

Are You a Believer Who Seeks?

CHAPTER 4

Are You a Believer Who Seeks?

"Do not merely listen to the word, and so deceive yourselves. Do what it says." - James 1:22

"And he died for all, that those who live should no longer live for themselves but for him who died for them and was raised again." - 2 Corinthians 5:15

Apply, don't simply hear. This goes back to the beginning of our read. If we are to seek God with all our hearts, minds, and souls, let it be our constant need and dependency on Him and not of ourselves. To listen to the word once a week at church, or to pick the Bible up from time to time is not enough to then apply your true dependency on God. My dad always taught me, "if you're going to talk the talk, then walk the walk". This is a way of life! We are so easily persuaded by our own desires and excuses that we simply choose to do what we want, when we want instead of truly allowing God to step in and direct us. God is calling for us daily. He is after our hearts, and wants to dive to the deepest part of our souls to know us, love us and guide us. He asks us to die to ourselves, so that we may become a reflection of Him. It's the only way to our eternal life with Him, there's no other way! You cannot earn your rights to Heaven, you cannot get into Heaven on your own accord, you cannot get into Heaven because you deem yourself a good person. You can only enter Heaven through believing and accepting God's son, Jesus Christ.

Not everyone who says to me, 'Lord, Lord,' will enter the kingdom of heaven, but only the one who does the will of my Father who is in heaven. Many will say to me on that day, 'Lord, Lord, did we not prophesy in your name and in your name drive out demons and in your name perform many miracles?' Then I will tell them plainly, 'I never knew you. Away from me, you evildoers!'" - Matthew 7:21-23

This is our book, Chapter 2: The Believer Not the Seeker Chapter 3: The Believer Who Seeks. The difference between true and false prophets. Which one are you? We are all on our own faith journey, I lived in chapter 2 most of my life. When I started living into chapter 3, that's when my life became fruitful and colorful. Unfortunately most Christians live worldly, and God tells us not to.

Jesus answered, "Very truly I tell you, no one can enter the kingdom of God unless they are born of water and the Spirit." - John 3:5

This is Jesus telling us, that unless we are born again through Him, meaning we must die to ourselves, we will not enter the Kingdom of God. We have a free gift and it's called salvation. This gift cannot be earned. It cannot be something you work for and then receive. It is free. The Holy Spirit has been placed in you through the acceptance of your free gift. Jesus is the light, the truth, and the way. There's no other way around it except through Him. We must desire a deepened relationship with Jesus if we want to know Him better. If your desires overpower His, then Satan wins. For every time you turn to yourself, you're creating a habit of self-dependency. It's easy to do, just like it is to get out of a good habit of eating healthy, exercising, getting enough sleep, spending quality time with your family. These are all choices, and instilled habits. They don't just naturally happen. If we are to truly be representatives of Christ, we're going to have to make some bold choices and changes to our lives. Many Christians have this idea that they will be missing out on life when they choose God. That very feeling is you dying to your flesh, your earthly body, your sinful nature. It may feel that way for a moment, but when you surrender that worldly idea and ask for Gods help, he will fill you with His truth, and His truth will set you free!

Obedience Over Sacrifice

Sprinkled throughout the Bible you will see the phrase obedience over sacrifice many times.

> ***"Does the Lord delight in burnt offerings and sacrifices as much as in obeying the voice of the Lord? To obey is better than sacrifice, and to heed is better than the fat of rams. For rebellion is like the sin of deviation (witchcraft) and arrogance like the evil of idolatry." - Samuel 15:22,23***

OBEDIENCE IF FAR BETTER THAN SACRIFICE.

> ***"For I desire mercy, not sacrifice, and acknowledgement of God rather than burnt offerings." - Hosea 6:6***

God doesn't want sacrifices; he wants our love and our loyalty. He doesn't want our rituals; he wants our hearts. We as Christians can get caught up in our routine of doing "Godly works" but deep down we're just going through the motions and there's no true joy in seeking God through it. We may go to church, volunteer at the services, host bible studies, and preach the gospel. However, most us go home and don't apply any of what we've learned. The question is, are we doing this from a place seeking to know God better, seeking to love and be obedient in drawing closer to him, or are we doing this as a robotic drill, a self-seeking place to find righteousness in ourselves? Are we going to church to learn His word and meditate on His truth? Are we conversing with God, and having conversation with God to understand His word and His truth? Are we then applying what we've heard, what we've read, what we've conversed with, thought about, meditated over and over and then put it into action? God doesn't want our repentance to be a replacement of doing good works. If our inward action and attitude are not right, than what's it matter to God if our outward action looks good? You cannot please God by looking Godly, you have to act Godly. God want's us to be in close relationship with Him. When you're obedient in following Him, God can then work boldly in your life. Ask God to create a pure heart and spirit in you, so that you may learn how to love Him more and seek Him more in obedience to His will for your life.

How To Hear God

How do you know it's God? Gods voice, the Holy Spirit within you will never contradict God's word. That's why reading His word is a key component to knowing God. The more time you spend in His word, the Bible, the more you will come to know His voice through His words. God may speak to you through dreams, visions, or your thoughts. He may use particular events, or circumstances to reach you or to confirm an earlier thought or vision. He also uses people to speak into us through Him. Ever have a thought hit you, whether it's someone to reach out to or a great idea, and then following that there's some sort of confirmation? Maybe that friend calls you first, or you see an event pop up that has to do with your idea, or a friend starts to talk to you

GOD DOESN'T WANT OUR REPENTANCE TO BE A REPLACEMENT OF DOING GOOD WORKS about what's been on your heart…that's God talking to you. The most important step after that is being obedient and following through even if it doesn't make sense or add up. Even if you think it's crazy, or stupid, or it could never happen! This is the action of faith, and faith will open doors in bigger ways than you could ever open for yourself. It's trusting that God will work all things out for your good and for His glory. God is always seeking us, but it is when we seek Him that we start to see how present and alive He is in our lives and how clear His direction is when we lean on Him instead of our own understanding. We can do nothing on our own, but with Christ we can do anything!

> ***"I can do all this through him who gives me strength." - Philippians 4:13***

Rest Assured

For the believer not the seeker, it's okay to wrestle with God. We all have our moments of doubt, insecurities, questions, and pain.

If you're going to challenge God based off those concerns, do it willingly to draw closer to Him and to know Him better.

GOD IS ALWAYS SEEKING US, BUT IT IS WHEN WE SEEK HIM THAT WE START TO SEE HOW PRESENT AND ALIVE HE IS IN OUR LIVES AND HOW CLEAR HIS DIRECTION IS WHEN WE LEAN ON HIM INSTEAD OF OUR OWN UNDERSTANDING

The ultimate place to live is in a place of hope, love, and redemption and that is the definition of Jesus. That is what He has to offer us. There's nothing more you need to do to be able to receive what Christ is offering. The gift of salvation is free to all who believe. The message I hope you take from this book, is no matter how you look at it, there are always two paths and two choices in life. Even as a believer, we have the choice to find freedom in Christ, to walk by faith with Him, trust in Him, and seek Him. We also have the choice to believe in Him, lack the confidence in Him, and question Him, thus the result of a self-depending, solo role. No matter which path we're on, we all will meet God face to face.

" For we must all appear before the judgment seat of Christ, so that each of us may receive what is due us for the things done while in the body, whether good or bad." - 2 Corinthians 5:10

Both believers and non-believers will have the opportunity to meet Christ. Unfortunately, some will not enter His Kingdom of Heaven. We know that walking with Christ is a narrow path, it is not the norm, it is not what the "cool" kids are doing. It's not the most popular or sought- after thing this world is yearning for.

> ***"Enter through the narrow gate. For wide is the gate and broad is the road that leads to destruction, and many enter through it. But small is the gate and narrow the road that leads to life, and only a few find it." - Matthew 7:13-14***

Doing the right thing isn't always the easiest. Showing love to your enemies, and forgiving those who have hurt you, is not the easiest. Saying you're sorry, admitting you're wrong, choosing to be the bigger person, is not the easiest. God is building your character so he can see you through Jesus, not of your own self. This is the narrow road that many will never find and the reason they'll never find it is because it is too hard, and too difficult, to do it on their own, they need Jesus.

Good News

There is good news though.

> ***"For God did not send his Son into the world to condemn the world, but to save the world through him." - John 3:17***

Jesus is our redeemer, and we can rest in knowing He came to save us, all of us. The path you choose is completely up to you. I know that with God's help you can choose the narrow path. This is all part of your faith journey. We will continue to grow in our faith and our walk with Christ until our time has come. We will have moments like David,

Solomon, Peter, Moses, and more when we shift our eyes off Christ and get distracted by the world or ourselves. In this moment in your life, the choice to not seek God will eventually lead you down a separate path away from God. It's not to say you don't believe in God or you don't love God, but be cautious on this path, for it is easy to lead you astray, replacing God with yourself, or the things of this world. Anything that does not lean toward God, will be a separate path and a separate journey on your own. My non-believer friends ask me if there is such a place as hell and if God is so loving why would he create a hell? I simply say, "All I know, is if God is everything good, and everything light, then hell is the opposite. It's everything wicked, everything evil, and everything dark. It's a separation from God and you have a choice. Be with God or be without God." God never intended for any of his children to go to hell, this was the consequence of our own choices. With our free will, and our free minds, we can choose God or ourselves. I encourage you to grow deeper in your relationship with Christ and allow him to be the center of your life. As you draw closer through prayer, and time spent in His word and loving His people, you will find God, and you will see he's been with you the whole time. There's a beautiful poem, I'm sure you've read it before, reminding us that God is always with us even when we don't feel him nearby:

One night I dreamed I was walking
along the beach with the Lord.
Many scenes from my life flashed across the sky.
In each scene I noticed footprints in the sand.
Sometimes there were two sets of footprints,
other times there were one set of footprints.
This bothered me because I noticed that
during the low periods of my life, when I was
suffering from anguish, sorrow, or defeat,
I could see only one set of footprints.
So I said to the Lord, "You promised me
Lord, that if I followed you,
you would walk with me always.
But I have noticed that during the most trying periods
of my life there have only been
one set of footprints in the sand.
Why, when I needed you most,
you have not been there for me?"
The Lord replied,
"The times when you have
seen only one set of footprints,
is when I carried you."

– Mary Stevenson

May we, as followers of Christ, embrace our journey of faith with grace, strength, and humility, trusting in the transformative power of God's perfect love to guide us on our spiritual mission in knowing Him and finding Him. God will always meet us where we are at, trust that He knows best and rest in His truth and His love for you.

Prayers Of Encouragement and Empowerment

Dear Lord,
Thank you for all your goodness in my life. Lord, I ask for you to reveal yourself to me in a mighty way. Help me seek you and know you. Help me surrender my heart and my life over to you daily. Help me trust you and walk by faith. Allow me to let go of my will and depend on your will for my life. Help me in the ways known and unknown to me that will align my life with you. I give all this to you in Jesus name.
Amen

Dear Heavenly Father,
Thank you for your righteousness and your plans for my life. I surrender my will to you right now. Lord I ask for the Armor of the Lord to come upon me, protect my mind, my heart, my spirit, my soul, and my body against the things that are not of you. Keep my eyes focused on you and your truth. Keep my feet grounded in your Word and your will for my life. I ask for forgiveness over the things I've done or said that are not in alignment with you and I ask for your help to turn away from those things. Grant me grace, peace, patients, and love the kind only you can give me to be a light to others. I bind anything that is not of you in the name of Jesus, and I take authority over my life and the plans you have for me. In Jesus name.
Amen

Dear Lord,
Thank you for being such a good God. Help me seek you and know you better. Grant me the wisdom and strength to walk in the ways of your council. All the things that are in my heart that I desire Lord, I surrender them over to you now and ask if it is your will that it will be done. I thank you in advance for taking care of my needs. Help me trust you as I let go of my own control and give it over to you. Allow my heart to soften so I can hear you and know you better. Grant me the spiritual eyes to see the truth in every and all situations known or unknown to me. I surrender all my burdens, all my questions, my doubts, my fears, and concerns over to you now. In Jesus name.
Amen

A book which I highly recommend adding to your reading list: ***The Rules of Engagement*** by Cindy Trimm. One of my favorite decrees from her book:

"I decree and declare that by the anointing, all covenants, contracts, chains, fetters, bondages, proclivities, and captivities that are contrary to, oppose, or hinder the fulfillment of God's original plan and purpose are broken. I am liberated from generational/ satanic/ demonic alliances,allegiances, soul ties, spirits of inheritance, and curses. I sever them by the sword of the Lord, the blood, and the Spirit. I speak to my DNA and declare that I am free from any and all influences passed down from one generation to another--biologically, socially, emotionally, physiologically, psychologically, spiritually, or by any other channel unknown to me but known to God. I resist every spirit that acts as a gatekeeper or a doorkeeper to my soul, and I renounce any further conscious or unconscious alliance, association, allegiance, or covenant. I open myself to divine deliverance. Father, have Your way now! Perfect those things concerning me".

(Deut. 5:9; 7:8-9; Eccles. 7:26; Isa. 61:1; Acts 8:9-13; Gal. 5:1; 1 Thess. 5:23-24;2 Tim. 2:25).

Take back your authority, use it and pray daily! Remember that you have the same authority and power that Jesus had. When Jesus died for our sins and rose on the third day, he left us with his Holy Spirit. The name of Jesus is the most powerful name in the world, even demons flee! So, use His name, and the authority that has been given to you through and in the name of Jesus.

"I have given you authority to trample on snakes and scorpions and to overcome all the power of the enemy; nothing will harm you." - Luke 10:19

"The seventy-two returned with joy and said, "Lord, even the demons submit to us in your name." - Luke 10:17

"You believe that there is one God. Good! Even the demons believe that—and shudder." - James 2:19

ABOUT THE AUTHOR

Rebekah Van Natta was born on January 27th, 1989. She is a wife, stepmother, soon to be mother (Expected Date: August 6th, 2024), identical twin and an entrepreneur. Rebekah is a paradigm of versatility and devotion - an entrepreneur, fitness enthusiast and athlete, Owner of RVNFIT- Personal Training and Integrated Reflexology, Real Estate Agent with Entity Mortgage and Realty (her husband's Brokerage), President and Founder of a 501(c)(3) nonprofit called The Stride Project, Part Owner and Founder of Lord and Armor, Part Owner and Founder of Savior Water, and a believer in Christ. Her journey, marked by passion and perseverance, began in earnest when she launched her personal training and reflexology business RVNFIT, in 2015 at the age of 25. This venture not only showcased her entrepreneurial spirit but also her dedication to health and wellness. Alongside her husband, Andy Martinez, Rebekah ventured into the realm of real estate to help her husband in opening his own Real Estate Brokerage where Andy focuses on the Mortgage side and Rebekah handles the Real Estate side. As a formidable team, they steer their company Entity Mortgage and Realty, assisting clients in buying, selling, and refinancing homes.

Their partnership extends beyond business, reflecting a shared vision and mutual respect. However, it's in her philanthropic endeavors where Rebekah's heart truly shines. Together with her twin sister, Rachel, she founded The Stride Project. This nonprofit intertwines fitness with charitable causes, specifically aiding cancer patients and their families. Through fitness challenges and events, the Stride Project raises funds, offering financial support and a message of hope to those battling cancer. Rebekah's faith in Christ is the cornerstone of her life, a guiding light that has led to the establishment of Lord and Armor. This venture, embodying her spiritual beliefs, publishes books like the one you're reading and runs an apparel line. Each piece of clothing is not just a fashion statement but a testament to her faith.

In her latest entrepreneurial endeavor, Rebekah and Andy introduced Savior Water. This canned water company is unique in its mission: donating 10% of profits to charities within the United States. Savior Water is more than a product; it's a symbol of hope and generosity, an extension of Rebekah's commitment to spreading the light of Jesus. On a personal front, Rebekah is an accomplished triathlete and ½ marathon runner. Her physical endurance and strength are paralleled by her mental resilience. Currently expecting her first child, due in August, she eagerly anticipates motherhood. Yet, even with this significant life change, she is determined to return to compete competitively in triathlons after her baby arrives. Rebekah's life transformed dramatically one year ago (2023) when she received Jesus as her Lord and Savior. The impact of this decision was profound, guiding her through various ventures and life choices. She attributes her success and direction to her unwavering faith in God, believing firmly that this is the path He has chosen for her. In this book "The Growing Christian: Two Paths to the Christian Belief," Rebekah aspires to capture the essence of her faith journey. Her story is one of continuous growth and exploration, a testament to living a life anchored in faith while pursuing diverse passions. Rebekah's journey is an inspiration, a reminder that with faith, determination, and compassion, one can lead a life that is not only fulfilling but also immensely impactful by the grace of God.

Get Involved!

To find out more about Rebekah's businesses continue reading:

Lord and Armor:

www.lordandarmor.com

Meet Andy and Rebekah, the dynamic duo behind Lord and Armor. As a devoted couple who share a deep love for the Lord, their journey of faith has been the driving force behind the creation of Lord and Armor Apparel. Inspired by their own spiritual journey and their desire to deepen their relationship with God, Andy and Rebekah felt compelled to share their faith with others. They envisioned Lord and Armor not just as a clothing brand, but as a platform to spread the message of Jesus Christ to believers and non-believers alike. More than just apparel, Lord and Armor is a testament to faith and courage. Each piece is carefully designed to ignite confidence and serve as a daily reminder of resilience and the right to stand out from the crowd. Join Andy and Rebekah on their mission to embrace the truth of Jesus while expressing your unique style and strength. Welcome to the family!

Savior Water

www.drinksaviorwater.com

John 4:14

"but whoever drinks the water I give them will never be thirsty again. But the water that I will give them will become in them a spring of water welling up to eternal life."

Every can of our Savior Water's got this really cool image of Christ on it. It's not just a picture; it feels like a beacon of hope, like He's offering this promise of something much bigger and better – His living water. It's like He's reaching out, not just offering a path to something eternal, but also kind of nudging us to think about others, to share what we've got with those who need a hand. Spiritually Rich, Ethically Committed.

Adorned with the words of John 4:14, every can of Savior Water is imbued with a commitment to faith and purity. This is hydration with a higher purpose – a connection between physical well-being and spiritual enrichment.

Tithing: Our Commitment to Giving Back

At Savior Water, tithing is at the heart of what we do. It's about taking that traditional step of giving back 10%, a value we hold dear. With every purchase of Savior Water, we're dedicating 10% of our earnings to uplift communities. This is more than a business model; it's our way of weaving generosity into every can. We're teaming up with inspiring American Christian organizations, spreading hope and offering support for fresh starts. Additionally, we're honoring our nation's heroes through contributions to organizations like the Wounded Warrior Project and Homes for Our Troops. Every can of Savior Water represents a commitment to this cycle of giving – it's our way of ensuring each sip carries a ripple effect of positive change. Your choice to pick up a can of Savior Water isn't just a refreshing choice, it's a step towards supporting a greater cause.

Our Cans: Eco-Friendly with a Touch of Heaven

We've put a lot of love into designing our Savior Water cans. They're not just earth-friendly, but they also carry a slice of heaven. Each can, with its radiant design featuring Christ, is like a little beacon of light and life. We like to think every sip shares a bit of that peace and purity.

Sipping on Faith, One Can at a Time

Savior Water is all about more than just quenching your thirst. It's like sowing seeds of faith wherever we go. Our goal is to reach out, especially to those who haven't found their faith yet, offering a little taste of Christ's love and the calmness that comes from His teachings.

Savior Water: More Than Just Hydration

When you pick up a can of Savior Water, you're joining something bigger. You are fighting the good fight. Go ahead, drink up the goodness and embrace the message. We're on this journey together to share the promise of living water and eternal life that Christ offers.

The Stride Project

www.thestrideproject.org

The Stride Project is a nonprofit organization dedicated to enhancing the quality of life for cancer patients and their families through a combination of fundraising and fitness challenges.

Our organization offers opportunities for individuals to make a meaningful impact. Volunteers are encouraged to participate in programs tailored to the specific needs of families, contingent on their geographical location. Additionally, we extend an invitation to those who wish to contribute to our mission by harnessing the power of fundraising through our dedicated platform, Pledge It. By engaging in active challenges, both individuals and teams have the chance not only to test their physical limits but also to participate in purpose-driven training and racing.

We have seamlessly integrated our fundraising platform with Strava, a complimentary fitness training application. This synchronization streamlines the process, automatically connecting your training progress to your personalized fundraising page. We encourage you to share your journey with friends and family, thereby involving a broader community in your dual mission: strengthening and challenging yourself, while also providing essential support to the families we assist. The financial resources raised are directed towards sponsored families who have shared their stories with us. These funds are allocated to address their unique and pressing needs during this transformative and challenging period.

If you are aware of a family in need of our support, we kindly ask you to submit their information to **rebekah@thestrideproject.org** . By doing so, you can help us extend our reach and offer assistance to those who can benefit from our services.

Sources:

https://www.bibletools.org/index.cfm/fuseaction/topical.show/RTD/cgg/ID/706/Separation-
from-God.htm

https://www.christwaycounseling.com/forms-resources/49-character-qualities-of-christ.php

https://compass1.org/2021/10/01/4-reasons-it-is-more-blessed-to-give-than-
receive/#:~:text="Remember%20the%20words%20of%20the,(Acts%2020%3A35).&text=Above%20all%20else%2C%20giving%20draws%20our%20heart%20to%20Christ.

https://www.jesusglitter.com/2018/05/03/you-dont-have-to-carry-the-weight-of-the-world/

https://www.symbis.com/blog/how-to-love-like-jesus/

https://www.christianity.com/wiki/christian-life/what-are-spiritual-gifts-understanding-the-types-and-discovering-yours.html

Romans 8 NIV - Life Through the Spirit - Therefore, - Bible Gateway

The Handbook For Spiritual Warfare- Dr. Ed Murphhy

Finding God- Dr. Larry Crabb

The Bible- NIV